ArchiMate® 4 Specification – A Pocket Guide

The Open Group Publications available from Van Haren Publishing

The TOGAF® Standard, 10th Edition:
Introduction and Core Concepts
Architecture Development Method
Content, Capability, and Governance
Leader's Guide
ADM Practitioners' Guide
Business Architecture
Enterprise Agility and Digital Transformation
A Pocket Guide
TOGAF® Business Architecture Foundation Study Guide
TOGAF® Enterprise Architecture Foundation Study Guide
TOGAF® Enterprise Architecture Practitioner Study Guide

The TOGAF Series (Version 9.2):
The TOGAF® Standard, Version 9.2
The TOGAF® Standard, Version 9.2 – A Pocket Guide
TOGAF® 9 Foundation Study Guide, 4th Edition
TOGAF® 9 Certified Study Guide, 4th Edition

The Open Group Series:
The IT4IT™ Standard, Version 3.0
IT4IT™ for Managing the Business of IT – A Management Guide
IT4IT™ Foundation Study Guide, 2nd Edition
The IT4IT™ Reference Architecture, Version 2.1 – A Pocket Guide
Cloud Computing for Business – The Open Group Guide
ArchiMate® 3.1 Specification – A Pocket Guide
ArchiMate® 3.2 Specification
ArchiMate® 4 Specification
ArchiMate® 4 Specification – A Pocket Guide
The Digital Practitioner Pocket Guide
The Digital Practitioner Foundation Study Guide
Open Agile Architecture™ – A Standard of The Open Group
Open Agile Architecture™ Standard, Version 2.0
Open Agile Architecture™ Standard, Version 2.0 – A Pocket Guide
Hospital Reference Architecture Guide: The Complete and Expanded English Translation of the Dutch ZiRA

The Open Group Press:
The Turning Point: A Novel about Agile Architects Building a Digital Foundation
Managing Digital
Ecosystems Architecture
For Your Information – About Information, the Universe, and the Modern Age

The Open Group Security Series:
O-TTPS™ – A Management Guide
Open Information Security Management Maturity Model (O-ISM3)
Open Enterprise Security Architecture (O-ESA)
Risk Management – The Open Group Guide
The Open FAIR™ Body of Knowledge – A Pocket Guide

All titles are available to purchase from:
www.opengroup.org
www.vanharen.net
and also many international and online distributors.

ArchiMate® 4 Specification

A POCKET GUIDE

THE Open GROUP

Van Haren
PUBLISHING

Title:	ArchiMate 4 Specification – A Pocket Guide
Series:	The Open Group Series
A Publication of:	The Open Group
Publisher:	Van Haren Publishing, 's-Hertogenbosch, www.vanharen.net
ISBN Paperback:	978 94 018 1480 5
ISBN eBook (pdf):	978 94 018 1481 2
ISBN ePub:	978 94 018 1482 9
Edition:	Fifth edition, first impression, April 2026
Layout:	The Open Group

Document Number: G265
Published by The Open Group, April 2026.

Comments relating to the material contained in this document may be submitted to:
The Open Group
Apex Plaza
Reading
Berkshire, RG1 1AX
United Kingdom
or by electronic mail to: ogspecs@opengroup.org

Table of Contents

Preface

The Open Group

The Open Group is a global consortium that enables the achievement of business objectives through technology standards and open source initiatives by fostering a culture of collaboration, inclusivity, and mutual respect among our diverse group of 900+ memberships. Our membership includes customers, systems and solutions suppliers, tool vendors, integrators, academics, and consultants across multiple industries.

The mission of The Open Group is to drive the creation of Boundaryless Information Flow™ achieved by:

- Working with customers to capture, understand, and address current and emerging requirements, establish policies, and share best practices
- Working with suppliers, consortia, and standards bodies to develop consensus and facilitate interoperability, to evolve and integrate specifications and open source technologies
- Offering a comprehensive set of services to enhance the operational efficiency of consortia
- Developing and operating the industry's premier certification service and encouraging procurement of certified products

Further information on The Open Group is available at www.opengroup.org.

The Open Group publishes a wide range of technical documentation, most of which is focused on development of Open Group Standards and Guides, but which also includes white papers, technical studies, certification and testing documentation, and business titles. Full details are available at www.opengroup.org/library.

This Document

This is the Pocket Guide to the ArchiMate® 4 Specification, a standard of The Open Group. It is intended to help architects by providing a reference for the ArchiMate graphical modeling language and to assist managers in understanding the basics of the ArchiMate language.

The intended audience of this document is Enterprise Architects, Business Architects, IT architects, Application Architects, Data Architects, Software Architects, Systems Architects, Solutions Architects, Infrastructure Architects, Process Architects, Domain Architects, Product Managers, Operational Managers, and Senior Managers seeking a first introduction to the ArchiMate modeling language

After reading this document, the reader seeking further information should refer to the ArchiMate documentation available online at www.opengroup.org/archimate.

This document is organized as follows:

- Chapter 1, *Introduction*, provides a high-level introduction to the ArchiMate Specification, its relationship to Enterprise Architecture, and an overview of changes in this version of the specification
- Chapter 2, *Language Structure*, describes the structure of the ArchiMate modeling language, including the top-level structure, aspects, domains, the ArchiMate core language, and the ArchiMate full language
- Chapter 3, *Common Domain*, describes the structure of the common, generic ArchiMate elements
- Chapter 4, *Relationships and Junctions*, describes the relationships in the language
- Chapter 5, *Motivation Domain*, describes the concepts for expressing the motivation for an architecture, together with examples
- Chapter 6, *Strategy Domain*, provides elements for modeling the enterprise at a strategic level, together with examples

- Chapter 7, *Business Domain*, covers the definition and usage of the Business Domain elements, together with examples
- Chapter 8, *Application Domain*, covers the definition and usage of the Application Domain elements, together with examples
- Chapter 9, *Technology Domain*, covers the definition and usage of the Technology Domain elements, together with examples
- Chapter 10, *Relationships Between Core Domains*, covers the relationships between different domains of the language
- Chapter 11, *Implementation and Migration Domain*, describes the language elements for expressing the implementation and migration aspects of an architecture (e.g., projects, deliverables, and plateaus)
- Chapter 12, *Architecture Views and Viewpoints*, describes the ArchiMate viewpoint mechanism, and the example viewpoints provided with the standard
- Appendix A, *Language Notation Summary*, is an informative appendix
- Appendix B, *Referenced Documents*, lists the publications referenced in this document
- Appendix C, *Glossary*, contains the glossary of terms for this document

Conventions Used in this Document

The following conventions are used throughout this document in order to help identify important information and avoid confusion over the intended meaning:

- Ellipsis (...)

  Indicates a continuation; such as an incomplete list of example items, or a continuation from preceding text.

- **Bold**

  Used to highlight specific terms.

- *Italics*

  Used for emphasis. May also refer to other external documents.

In addition to typographical conventions, the following conventions are used to highlight segments of text:

> **Note**
>
> A Note box is used to highlight useful or interesting information.

> **Tip**
>
> A Tip box is used to provide key information that can save you time or that may not be entirely obvious.

About the Authors

This document builds on materials from the ArchiMate® 4 Specification, published by The Open Group [C260]. The authors listed here have prepared this Pocket Guide which is intended to be a condensed reference for the ArchiMate modeling language. See Acknowledgements for more information.

Andrew Josey, The Open Group

Andrew Josey, a Fellow of The Open Group, is VP Standards and Certification overseeing all certification and testing programs of The Open Group. He also manages the standards process for The Open Group, and is Editor-in-Chief for The Open Group Publications.

Since joining the company in 1996, Andrew has been closely involved with the standards development, certification and testing activities of The Open Group. He has led many standards development projects including specification and certification development for the ArchiMate®, TOGAF®, POSIX®, and UNIX® programs.

He is a member of the IEEE, USENIX, and the Association of Enterprise Architects® (AEA). He holds an MSc in Computer Science from University College London.

Marc Lankhorst, Bizzdesign

As Managing Consultant and Chief Technology Evangelist at Bizzdesign, Marc Lankhorst contributes to Bizzdesign's vision, market development, consulting, and coaching on digital business design and Enterprise Architecture. His expertise and interests range from Enterprise Architecture and business process management to service orientation, Agile methods and digital business design.

Marc has been closely involved in the development of the ArchiMate® language for Enterprise Architecture modeling, a standard of The Open Group, and he leads the team that works on the further evolution of the standard. Based on this experience, he helps organizations with implementing and using the ArchiMate language in practice.

He is frequent speaker at conferences and the primary author of two books, "Enterprise Architecture at Work" and "Agile Service Development". Marc is ArchiMate®, TOGAF® 9, and IT4IT® certified, and holds an MSc in Computer Science from the University of Twente and a PhD from the University of Groningen in The Netherlands.

Henk Jonkers, Bizzdesign

Henk Jonkers is a Research Engineer, contributing to the development of enterprise modeling-related functionality in the Bizzdesign tool suite. In previous years, as a Professional Services Consultant, he delivered consultancy and training to customers in Enterprise Architecture and related areas, including Security Architecture and Capability-based planning.

Henk has been involved in the development of the ArchiMate language since the beginning and actively contributes to the activities of The Open Group ArchiMate Forum. He is ArchiMate® 3 and TOGAF® 9 certified, and holds an MSc in Computer Science from the University of Twente and a PhD from Delft University of Technology in The Netherlands.

Jean-Baptiste Sarrodie, BNP PARIBAS

Jean-Baptiste Sarrodie has been working in the field of IT as a manager and an architect in several industries for over 20 years. He now works as an enterprise architect for BNP PARIBAS bank and divides his time between accompanying the bank's transformation projects and working on the evolution of the ArchiMate® Specification within The Open Group.

Since 2013, Jean-Baptiste has been contributing to the development of the open source modelling tool, Archi. Jean-Baptiste is also Chair of The Open Group ArchiMate Forum

Trademarks

ArchiMate, FACE, FACE logo, Future Airborne Capability Environment, Making Standards Work, Open Footprint, Open O logo, Open O and Check certification logo, Open Subsurface Data Universe, OSDU, Sensor Open Systems Architecture, SOSA, SOSA logo, The Open Group, TOGAF, UNIX, UNIXWARE, and X logo are registered trademarks and Boundaryless Information Flow, Build with Integrity Buy with Confidence, Commercial Aviation Reference Architecture, Dependability Through Assuredness, Digital Practitioner Body of Knowledge, DPBoK, Eagle AI Assistant and logo, EMMM, FHIM Profile Builder, FHIM logo, FPB, IT4IT, IT4IT logo, O-AA, O-DA, O-DEF, O-HERA, O-PAS, O-TTPS, O-VBA, Open Agile Architecture, Open FAIR, Open Process Automation, Open Trusted Technology Provider, and Sensor Integration Simplified are trademarks of The Open Group.

Association of Enterprise Architects is a registered trademark of the Association of Enterprise Architects.

IBM is a registered trademark of International Business Machines Corp.

Java is a registered trademark of Oracle.

UML and Unified Modeling Language are registered trademarks of the Object Management Group.

All other brands, company, and product names are used for identification purposes only and may be trademarks that are the sole property of their respective owners.

Acknowledgements

The Open Group gratefully acknowledges The Open Group ArchiMate Forum for developing and maintaining the ArchiMate Specification.

The Open Group gratefully acknowledges the following reviewers who participated in the review of this document:

- Antonio Carlos Plais do Couto
- Max Hemingway
- Anshul Purohit

Chapter 1. Introduction

This chapter introduces the ArchiMate® Specification, a standard of The Open Group.

Topics addressed in this chapter include:

- An introduction to the ArchiMate Specification
- The ArchiMate language and its relationship to Enterprise Architecture
- The ArchiMate language and its relationship to the TOGAF® Standard

1.1. Introduction to the ArchiMate Specification

The ArchiMate Specification defines an open and independent modeling language for Enterprise Architecture that is supported by different tool vendors and consulting firms.

The ArchiMate language enables Enterprise Architects to describe, analyze, and visualize the relationships among architecture domains in an unambiguous way. It provides a uniform representation for diagrams that describe Enterprise Architectures, including concepts for specifying inter-related architectures, specific viewpoints for selected stakeholders, and language customization mechanisms.

This document is the Pocket Guide to the ArchiMate 4 Specification, referred to simply as the "ArchiMate Specification" within this document. The ArchiMate 4 Specification is a major release of the ArchiMate Specification. This Pocket Guide provides a quick reference to the concepts and elements of the ArchiMate language.

Development of the ArchiMate Language

The ArchiMate language was created in the period 2002-2004 in the Netherlands by a project team from the Telematica Instituut in cooperation with several partners from government, industry, and academia, including Ordina, Radboud Universiteit Nijmegen, the Leiden Institute for Advanced Computer Science (LIACS), and the Centrum Wiskunde & Informatica (CWI). The development included tests in organizations such as ABN AMRO, the Dutch Tax and Customs Administration, and the Stichting Pensioenfonds ABP. In 2008, the ownership and stewardship of the ArchiMate language was transferred from the ArchiMate Foundation to The Open Group. Since 2009, The Open Group ArchiMate Forum has developed successive versions and published them on The Open Group website.

1.2. The ArchiMate Language and Enterprise Architecture

The role of the ArchiMate Specification is to provide a graphical language for the representation of Enterprise Architecture over time (i.e., including strategic, transformation, and migration planning), as well as the motivation and rationale for the architecture. The ArchiMate modeling language provides a uniform representation for diagrams that describe Enterprise Architecture, and offers an integrated approach to describe and visualize the different architecture domains together with their underlying relations and dependencies.

The design of the ArchiMate language started from a set of relatively generic concepts (objects and relations), which have been specialized for application at the different architectural layers for an Enterprise Architecture. The most important design restriction on the ArchiMate language is that it has been explicitly designed to be as compact as possible, yet still functionable for most Enterprise Architecture modeling tasks. In the interest of simplicity of learning and use, the language has been limited to the concepts that suffice for modeling the proverbial 80% of practical cases.

1.3. The TOGAF Standard

The ArchiMate language complements the TOGAF Standard [C220] in that it provides a vendor-independent set of concepts, including a graphical representation, that helps to create a consistent, integrated model "below the waterline", which can be depicted in the form of TOGAF views.

The structure of the ArchiMate core language closely corresponds with the three main architectures as addressed in the TOGAF Architecture Development Method (ADM). The strategy, motivation, implementation, and migration elements approximately map onto the remainder of the ADM (although these elements may also be used in Phases B, C, and D). This is illustrated in Figure 1-1.

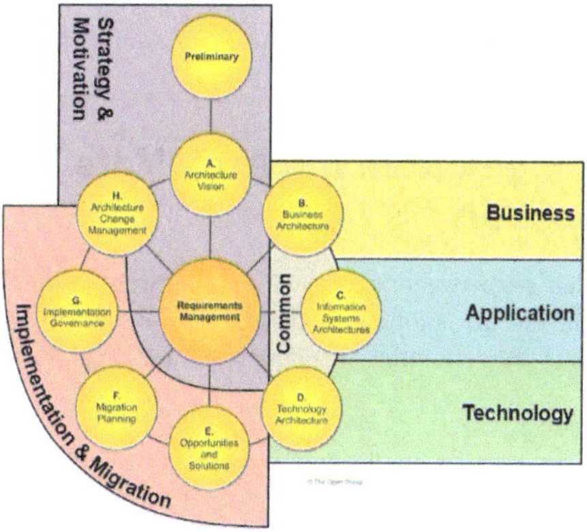

Figure 1-1: Correspondence Between the ArchiMate Language and the TOGAF ADM

This correspondence indicates a fairly easy mapping between TOGAF views and the ArchiMate viewpoints. A more detailed description of this correspondence is given in The Open Group Guide *How to Use the ArchiMate® Modeling Language to Support the TOGAF® Standard* [G21E].

It is important to reiterate that the ArchiMate Specification is a modeling language and not a framework. Therefore, the viewpoint definitions are more detailed and specify the stakeholders, concerns, level of detail, or abstraction level, and the entity types involved in the viewpoints. In the TOGAF Standard this is presented in a more general way. Therefore, some interpretation or transformation will be required.

In conclusion, the TOGAF Standard and the ArchiMate Specification can easily be used in conjunction:

- The two standards complement each other with respect to the definition of an architecture development process and the definition of an Enterprise Architecture modeling language
- The two standards overlap in their use of viewpoints, and the concept of an underlying common repository of architectural artifacts and models; i.e., they have a firm common foundation
- The combined use of the two standards can support a better communication with stakeholders

1.4. Changes from the ArchiMate 3.2 Specification

The main changes between Version 3.2 and the ArchiMate 4 Specification are listed below. In addition to these changes, various other minor improvements in definitions, explanations, and examples have been made:

- Business interaction, application interaction, technology interaction, constraint, contract, gap, and representation have been removed
- Behavior elements have been merged across layers, leading to a single set of service, process, function, and event
- Implementation event has been replaced by the now generic event element

- Business, application, and technology collaborations have been merged into a single collaboration element
- Business role has been replaced by a generic role element to which any internal active structure element can be assigned
- The depiction of the language has been updated and is no longer a matrix combining aspects and layers, but the "ArchiMate Hexagonion" (a concentric layered hexagon diagram)
- The term *layer* has been replaced by the more generic term *domain*
- The "Generic Metamodel" chapter has been replaced by a chapter describing all the previously mentioned generic elements
- Path is now a part of the Common Domain
- Aggregation from path to technology internal active structure element has been replaced by a realization from active structure element to path
- Relationships can now have multiplicity to express the constraints put on the instances of elements on their ends

ArchiMate 3.2 models can easily be translated to the new version by applying the following transformations:

- Constraint can be replaced by a (specialization of) requirement
- Contract can be replaced by a (specialization of) business object
- Gap can be replaced by a (specialization of) assessment or deliverable
- Representation can be replaced by a (specialization of) data object, artifact, or material
- Business, application, and technology interactions can be replaced by a (specialization of) function or process
- Other business, application, and technology behavior elements can be replaced by (a specialization of) their generic counterpart
- Implementation event can be replaced by a (specialization of) event
- If a relationship between two elements in a model is no longer permitted, replace it by an association

If it concerns an aggregation from a path to a technology internal active structure element, this may be replaced by a realization from the technology active structure element to the path. If it concerns a realization between services of different layers, this may be replaced by a specialization (from the realizing service to the realized service) or an aggregation (from the realized service to the realizing service).

Chapter 2. Language Structure

This chapter describes the structure of the ArchiMate Enterprise Architecture modeling language.

2.1. The ArchiMate Language

The concepts of the ArchiMate language are organized in domains and aspects.

2.1.1. Domains of the ArchiMate Language

The ArchiMate core language defines a set of domains with specific active, behavior, and passive structure elements. Four domains are defined within the ArchiMate core language as follows:

- The Common Domain (see Chapter 3) contains generic elements (in particular behavior elements) that can be used in combination with elements from different domains
- The Business Domain (see Chapter 7) depicts the organization, how it relates to its internal and external customers, and what it consumes and produces
- The Application Domain (see Chapter 8) depicts the applications, how they work together to support the business, and which data they process
- The Technology Domain (see Chapter 9) comprises both information technology and operational (physical) technology

Figure 2-1 depicts the contents of the core language.

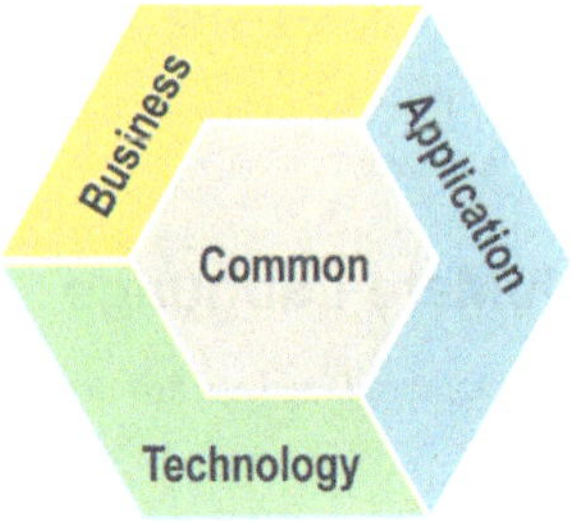

Figure 2-1: ArchiMate Core Language

Next to these core domains, the language also comprises:

- The Motivation Domain (see Chapter 5), containing elements to model stakeholders, goals, and other related contexts and motivations that drive the architecture
- The Strategy Domain (see Chapter 6), used to model strategic direction and choices, based on the motivation of the enterprise
- The Implementation and Migration Domain (see Chapter 11), with elements for modeling the evolution and implementation of architectures

The structure of the language allows for the modeling of the enterprise from different viewpoints, where a stakeholder can have concerns that cover multiple aspects and domains.

Figure 2-2 shows a symbolic representation of the full language. Intentionally, "Motivation" is put in the center, since it describes the goals that the architecture is aiming for. Working outward from the center, these goals are translated into high-level and more concrete architectural designs, and a plan for the implementation of those designs.

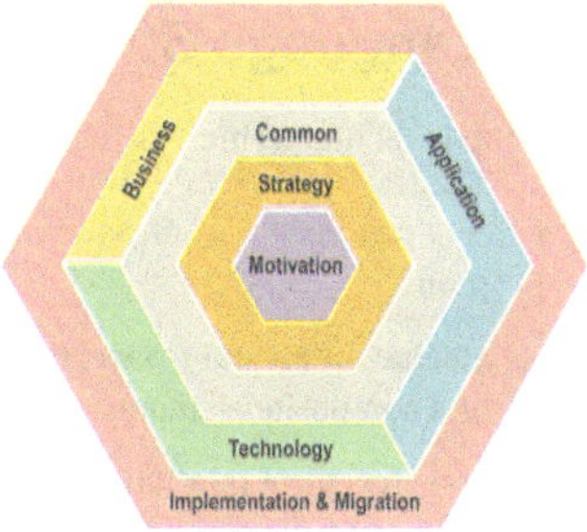

Figure 2-2: ArchiMate Full Language

2.1.2. Aspects of the ArchiMate Language

The three core aspects are:

- The *Active Structure Aspect*, which represents the structural elements (such as the business actors, application components, devices, and equipment that display actual behavior; i.e., the "subjects" of activity)
- The *Behavior Aspect*, which represents the behavior (processes, functions, events, and services) performed by the actors; structural elements are assigned to behavioral elements, to show who or what displays this behavior
- The *Passive Structure Aspect*, which represents the objects on which behavior is performed; these are usually information in the Business Domain and data in the Application Domain, but they may also be used to represent physical materials in the Technology Domain

These aspects were inspired by natural language, where a sentence has a subject (active structure), a verb (behavior), and an object (passive structure). By using the same constructs that people are used to in their own languages, the ArchiMate language is easier to learn and read.

A composite element, as shown in Figure 2-3, is an element that does not necessarily fit in a single aspect but may combine multiple aspects.

2.2. Top-Level Language Structure

Figure 2-3 outlines the top-level hierarchical structure of the language:

- A model is a collection of *concepts* — a concept is either an *element*, a *relationship*, or a *junction*
- An element is either a behavior element, a structure element, a motivation element, or a composite element
- A relationship is either a structural relationship, a dependency relationship, a dynamic relationship, or an other relationship

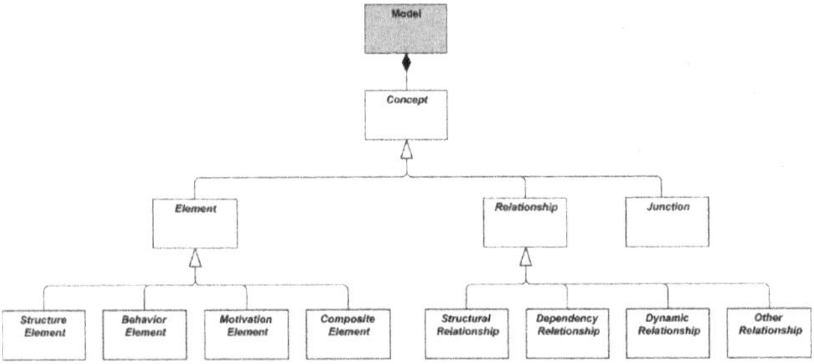

Figure 2-3: Top-Level Hierarchy of ArchiMate Concepts

2.3. Structure and Behavior Elements

The main hierarchy of behavior and structure elements of the ArchiMate language is presented in the metamodel fragment of Figure 2-4. It defines these elements in a generic, domain-independent way.

This generic metamodel fragment consists of two main types of elements: *structure* ("nouns") and *behavior* elements ("verbs").

Structure elements can be subdivided into *active structure* elements and *passive structure* elements. Active structure elements can be further divided into *external* active structure elements (also called *interfaces*) and *internal* active structure elements.

Behavior elements can be subdivided into *internal behavior* elements, *services (which equals external behavior element), and _event.*

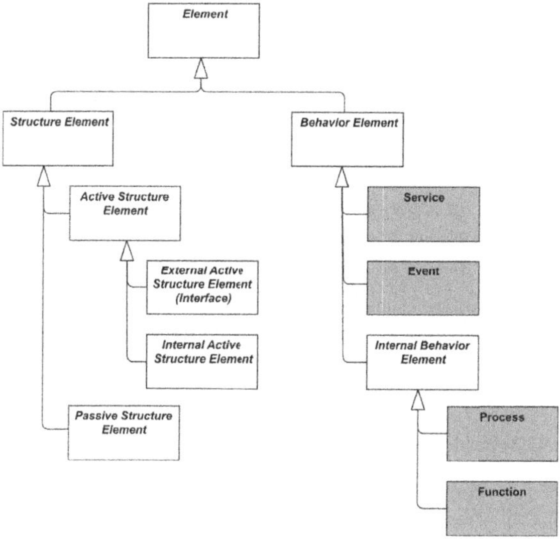

Figure 2-4: Hierarchy of Behavior and Structure Elements

2.3.1. Active Structure Elements

Active structure elements are the subjects that can perform behavior. These can be divided into internal active structure elements (the business actors, application components, nodes, etc.) that perform this behavior, and external active structure elements; i.e., the interfaces that expose this behavior to human consumers or non-human systems. An interface provides an external view on the service provider and hides its internal structure.

> An internal active structure element represents an entity that is capable of performing behavior.

An external active structure element, called an interface, represents a point of access where an internal active structure element makes one or more services available to its environment.

2.3.2. Passive Structure Elements

Passive structure elements can be accessed by behavior elements.

A passive structure element represents an element on which behavior is performed.

A passive structure element is a structural element that cannot perform behavior. Active structure elements can perform behavior on passive structure elements. Passive structure elements are often information or data objects, but they can also represent physical objects.

2.3.3. Behavior Elements

Behavior elements represent the dynamic aspects of an enterprise. Similar to active structure elements, behavior elements can be divided into *internal* behavior elements and services that are exposed to the environment.

An internal behavior element represents a unit of activity that can be performed by one or more internal active structure elements.

An external behavior element, called a service, represents an explicitly defined behavior, exposed to the environment.

2.3.4. Example

Example 2-1 illustrates both active structure and behavior elements. The internal active structure element "Finance" application component performs the internal behavior element "Transaction Processing" function. It aggregates the external active structure element "Payment Interface", which provides access to the service "Payment Service".

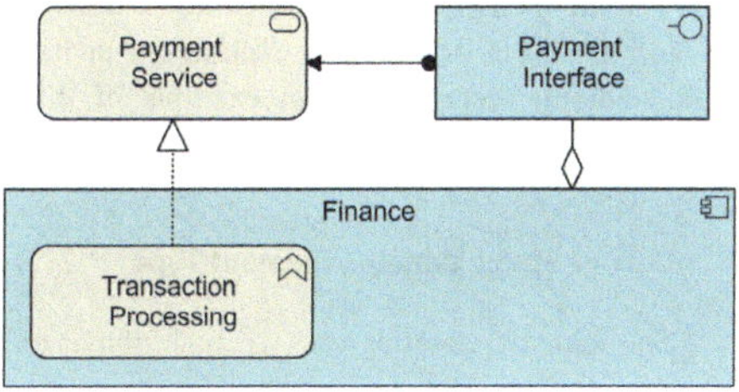

Example 2-1: Active Structure and Behavior Elements

2.4. Use of Colors and Notational Cues

In the metamodel pictures within this document, shades of gray are used to distinguish elements belonging to the different aspects of the ArchiMate language, as follows:

- White for abstract (i.e., non-instantiable) concepts
- Gray for concrete concepts

In ArchiMate models, there are no formal semantics assigned to colors and the use of color is left to the modeler. However, they can be used freely to stress certain aspects in models. For instance, in many of the example models presented in this document, colors are used to distinguish between the domains of the ArchiMate language, as follows:

- Purple for the Motivation Domain
- Orange for the Strategy Domain

- Warm gray for the Common Domain
- Yellow for the Business Domain
- Blue for the Application Domain
- Green for the Technology Domain
- Pink for the Implementation and Migration Domain

In addition to the colors, other notational cues can be used to distinguish between the domains of the language. A letter M, S, C, B, A, T, or I in the top-left corner of an element can be used to denote a Motivation, Strategy, Common, Business, Application, Technology, or Implementation and Migration element, respectively. An example of this notation is shown in Example 10-1.

Corner Shape denotes Element Type

The standard notation uses a convention as follows:

- Square corners denote structure elements
- Rounded corners denote behavior elements
- Diagonal corners denote motivation elements

Chapter 3. Common Domain

The common, generic concepts, which are used across different domains, are shown in Figure 3-1.

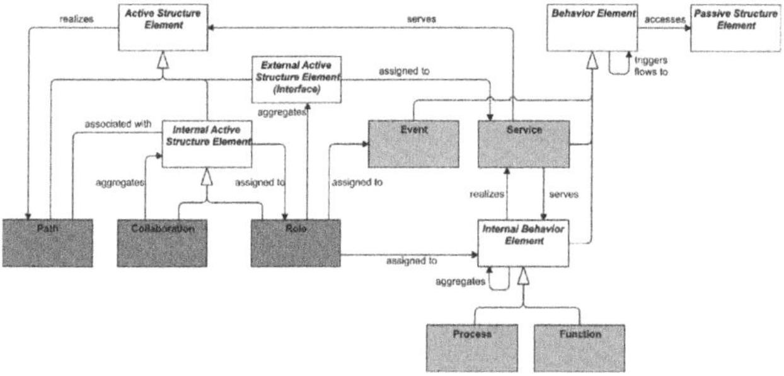

Figure 3-1: Common Domain Metamodel

3.1. Active Structure Elements

3.1.1. Role

> A role represents the position or purpose that a business actor, application component, node, device, system software, equipment, facility, or a collaboration has in performing specific behavior.

Roles with certain responsibilities or skills are assigned to processes or functions. In addition to the relation of a role with behavior, a role is also useful in a (structural) organizational sense; for instance, in the division of labor within an organization.

The name of a role should preferably be a noun. For example, a business actor can be assigned to a "Requester" or "Approver" role, or an application component can be assigned to a "Policy Enforcement Point" or "Policy Decision Point" role.

Figure 3-2: Role Notation

3.1.2. Collaboration

A collaboration represents a collection of business actors, application components, nodes, devices, system software, equipment, facilities, roles, and/or other collaborations that work together to perform collective behavior.

A collaboration is a (possibly temporary) collection of internal active structure elements (including other collaborations) which perform collaborative behavior. Unlike, say, a department, a collaboration need not have an official (permanent) status within the organization.

A collaboration may be assigned to one or more processes or functions. A collaboration may aggregate interfaces that it provides to its environment, and interfaces may serve a collaboration. The name of a collaboration should preferably be a noun.

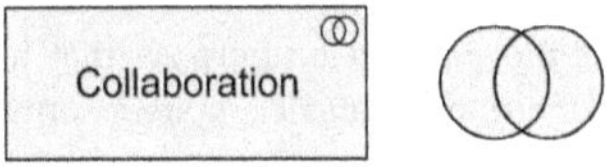

Figure 3-3: Collaboration Notation

3.1.3. Path

A path represents a logical link between business actors, application components, nodes, devices, system software, equipment, facilities, roles, and/or collaborations, through which these elements can exchange information, data, energy, or material.

A path is used to model the logical communication or distribution relations between internal active structure elements.

A path can be associated with the internal active structure elements it connects. Typical examples of paths are a Virtual Private Network (VPN), realized by WiFi, Local Area Network (LAN), and Wide Area Network (WAN) communication networks; intermodal freight, realized by a combination of shipping, trucking, and rail distribution networks; or a social network that lets users communicate with each other.

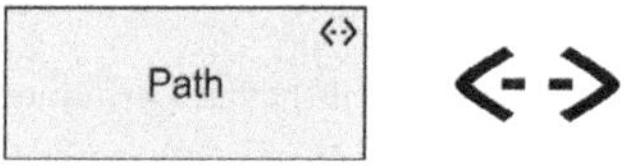

Figure 3-4: Path Notation

3.2. Behavior Elements

3.2.1. Service

> A service represents an explicitly defined behavior that a business actor, application component, node, device, system software, equipment, facility, role, or collaboration provides to its environment.

A service exposes specific functionality of the providing active structure element (for example, an organization unit or IT system) from the perspective of others that use that service; the environment consists of everything outside this providing organization unit or system.

The name of a service should clearly describe the functionality being offered (for example, using a verb ending with "-ing"); e.g., "claims processing", "transaction processing", or "messaging". Also, a name explicitly containing the word "service" may be used; e.g., "data replication service".

Figure 3-5: Service Notation

3.2.2. Process

> A process represents a sequence of behaviors that achieves a specific result.

A process describes the internal behavior performed by a role that is required to produce a set of services.

The name of a process should clearly indicate a predefined sequence of actions using a verb or verb-noun combination and may include the word "process". Examples are "adjudicate claim", "employee on-boarding", "approval process", "general ledger update job", or "replicate database".

Figure 3-6: Process Notation

3.2.3. Function

> A function represents a collection of behavior based on a chosen set of criteria.

Just like a process, a function also describes internal behavior performed by a role. However, while a process groups behavior based on a sequence or flow of activities that is needed to realize a product or service, a function typically groups behavior based on required resources, skills, competencies, knowledge, etc.

Organizational units or applications may coincide with functions due to their specific grouping of activities. In the Business Domain, functions are often closely aligned to an organization, but not necessarily explicitly governed by the organization.

The name of a function should clearly indicate a well-defined behavior, but unlike processes, it is typically not in the form of a verb-noun phrase. Examples are customer management, claims administration, recycling, or payment processing.

Figure 3-7: Function Notation

3.2.4. Event

> An event represents something that happens or occurs inside or outside the enterprise, such as a state change.

Processes and other behavior may be triggered or interrupted by an event. Processes may raise events that trigger other processes or functions. Unlike processes or functions, an event is instantaneous: it does not have a duration. Events may originate from the environment of the organization (e.g., from a customer) or some external physical or IT system, as well as internal events generated within the organization or system world.

An event may trigger or be triggered (raised) by a process or function. An event may access passive elements and may aggregate other events. The name of an event should preferably be a verb in the perfect tense; e.g., "Claim Received".

Figure 3-8: Event Notation

Example

"Claims Administration" is a function that aggregates a number of processes. This function realizes a "Claims Processing" service. An event "Claim Filed" triggers the first process "Accept Claim Risk", which in turn triggers a process "Assign Claim". Depending on the type of claim, either the process "Adjudicate Standard Claim" or the process "Adjudicate High-Risk Claim" is performed. According to the company policy, two roles should always be involved in the latter process, to minimize the risk of fraud. This is modeled with the collaboration "High-Risk Claims Adjudication". After adjudication, the processes "Notify Customer" and "Pay Claim" are performed in parallel, and when both have finished, process "Close Claim" is triggered.

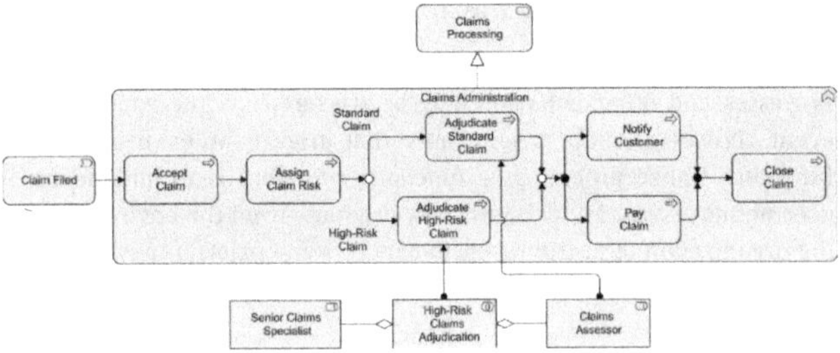

Example 3-1: Common Domain Elements

3.3. Composite Elements

3.3.1. Grouping

A grouping represents a collection of concepts that belong together based on some common characteristic.

The grouping element is used to aggregate an arbitrary group of concepts, which can be elements and/or relationships of the same or of different types.

Figure 3-9: Grouping Notation

Example

In Example 3-2, the "Grouping" element is used to aggregate a conglomerate of two processes and an object that together realize a service (both with nesting and explicitly drawn aggregation relationships).

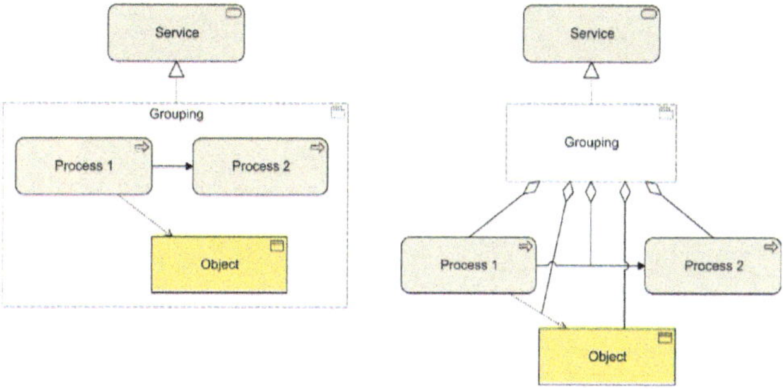

Example 3-2: Grouping

3.3.2. Location

A location represents a place or position where structure elements can be located or behavior can be performed.

The location element is used to model the place where (active and passive) structure elements such as business actors, application components, and devices are located. This covers both physical (e.g., geographical) locations and logical places such as the regions of cloud providers. This is modeled by means of an aggregation relationship from a location to structure element. A location can also aggregate a behavior element, to indicate where the behavior is performed.

Figure 3-10: Location Notation

3.4. Summary

Table 3-1 provides a summary of the common core elements, their definitions, and their default graphical notation.

Table 3-1: Common Core Elements

Element	Definition	Notation
Active Structure		
Role	The position or purpose that a business actor, application component, node, device, system software, equipment, facility, or a collaboration has in performing specific behavior.	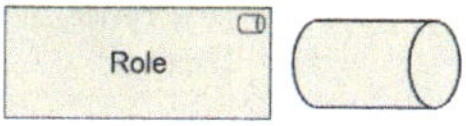
Collaboration	A collection of business actors, application components, nodes, devices, system software, equipment, facilities, roles, and/or other collaborations that work together to perform collective behavior.	
Path	A logical link between business actors, application components, nodes, devices, system software, equipment, facilities, roles, and/or collaborations, through which these elements can exchange data, energy, or material.	
Behavior		
Process	A sequence of behaviors that achieves a specific result.	
Function	A collection of behavior based on a chosen set of criteria.	

Element	Definition	Notation
Service	An explicitly defined behavior that a business actor, application component, node, device, system software, equipment, facility, role, or collaboration provides to its environment.	
Event	Something that happens or occurs inside or outside the enterprise, such as a state change.	
Composite		
Grouping	A collection of concepts that belong together based on some common characteristic.	
Location	A place or position where structure elements can be located or behavior can be performed.	

Chapter 4. Relationships and Junctions

In addition to the generic elements outlined in Chapter 3, the ArchiMate language defines a core set of generic relationships.

The relationships are classified as follows (see Figure 4-1):

- *Structural* relationships, which model the static construction or composition of concepts of the same or different types
- *Dependency* relationships, which model how elements are used to support other elements
- *Dynamic* relationships, which are used to model behavioral dependencies between elements
- *Other* relationships, which do not fall into one of the above categories

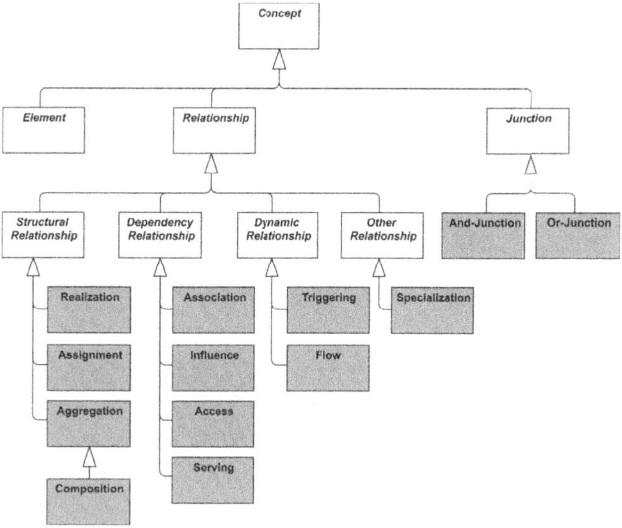

Figure 4-1: Overview of Relationships

Each relationship has exactly one "from" and one "to" concept (element, relationship, or junction) as endpoints. The following restrictions apply:

- No relationships are allowed between two relationships
- All relationships connected with the same junction must be of the same type
- A chain of relationships of the same type that connects two elements, and is in turn connected via junctions, is valid only if a direct relationship of that same type between those two elements is valid
- A relationship connecting an element with a second relationship can only be an aggregation or association; aggregation is valid only from a composite element to that second relationship

It is good practice to explicitly name or label any relationship that would otherwise be ambiguous or misunderstood.

4.1. Structural Relationships

Structural relationships represent the "static" coherence within an architecture.

4.1.1. Aggregation Relationship

An aggregation relationship represents that an element combines one or more other concepts.

The aggregation relationship has been inspired by the aggregation relationship in Unified Modeling Language® (UML®) class diagrams.

An aggregation relationship is always allowed between two elements of the same type.

In addition to this, the metamodel explicitly defines other source and target elements that may be connected by an aggregation relationship.

Figure 4-2: Aggregation Notation

Example

Example 4-1 shows two ways to express that the "Customer File" aggregates an "Insurance Policy" and "Claim".

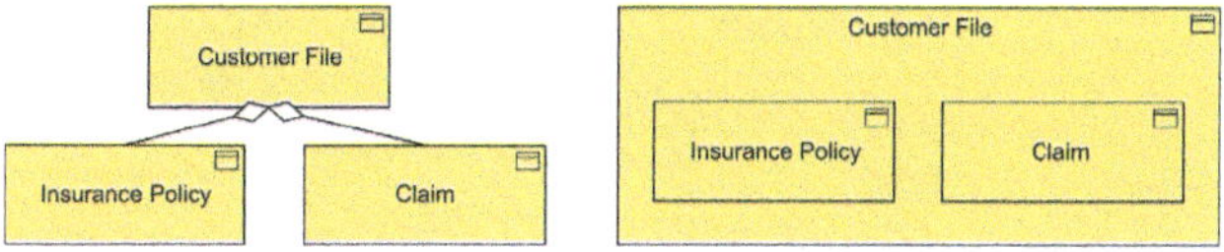

Example 4-1: Aggregation

4.1.2. Composition Relationship

> A composition relationship represents that an element combines one or more other concepts, where the existence of those concepts depends on that of the element.

The composition relationship is a specialization of the aggregation relationship that expresses an existence dependency: If a composite is deleted, its parts are deleted as well. When you model real-world elements (for example, an organization structure of departments and teams expressed as business actors), this dependency applies to these elements themselves.

A composition relationship is allowed in exactly the same cases where an aggregation relationship would be allowed. It follows the same semantics as aggregation relationships.

Figure 4-3: Composition Notation

Example

> Example 4-2 shows that the company "ArchiSurance" consists of "ArchiSurance Contact Center" and "ArchiSurance Back Office", which in turn consists of three departments.

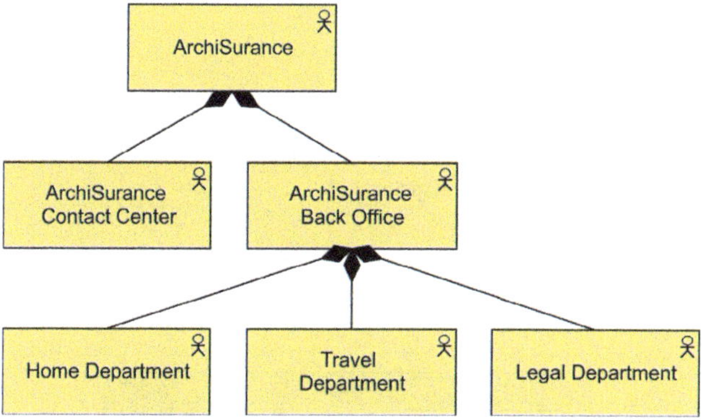

Example 4-2: Composition

4.1.3. Assignment Relationship

> An assignment relationship represents the allocation of responsibility, performance of behavior, storage, or execution.

The assignment relationship links active structure elements with units of behavior that are performed by them, internal active structure elements (e.g., business actors) with roles fulfilled by them, and active structure elements with passive structure elements from the same domain. It can, for example, relate an internal active structure element with an internal behavior element, an interface with a service, or a node, device, and system software with an artifact.

Figure 4-4: Assignment Notation

The interpretation of an assignment relationship is that the *whole or part* of the source element is assigned the *whole of* the target element.

Example

Example 4-3 includes the two ways to express the assignment relationship. The “Finance” application component is assigned to the “Transaction Processing” function, and the “Payment Interface” is assigned to the “Payment Service”.

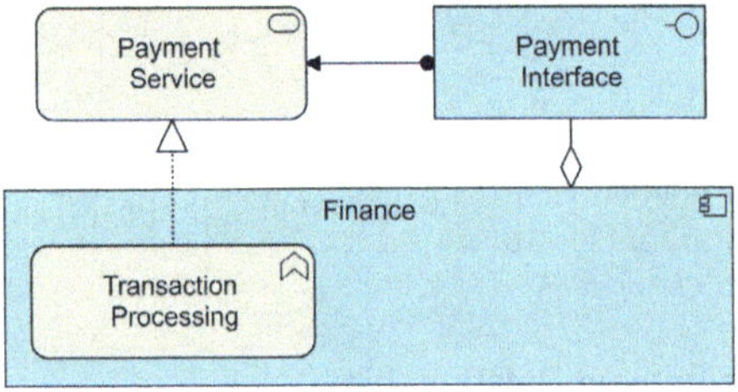

Example 4-3: Assignment

4.1.4. Realization Relationship

A realization relationship represents that an element plays a critical role in the creation, achievement, sustenance, or operation of a more abstract element.

A realization relationship indicates that more abstract elements (“what” or “logical”) are realized by means of more tangible elements (“how” or “physical”). The realization relationship is used to model run-time realization; for example, that a process realizes a service, and that a data object realizes a business object, an artifact realizes an application component, or a core element realizes a motivation element.

Figure 4-5: Realization Notation

The interpretation of a realization relationship is that the *whole or part* of the source element realizes the *whole of* the target element.

For realization, nesting as a notation is allowed in both directions of the relationship. For instance, a service can be nested in an application component to express that it is realized by that application component, and a process nested in a capability may express that this process realizes the capability. Since this can lead to ambiguity, it is advisable to use it only in one direction in the same view and add an explanation to any view in which such ambiguity may arise.

Example

Example 4-4 illustrates two ways to use the realization relationship. A "Transaction Processing" function realizes a "Billing Service"; the "Invoice" business object is realized by the data object "Billing Data".

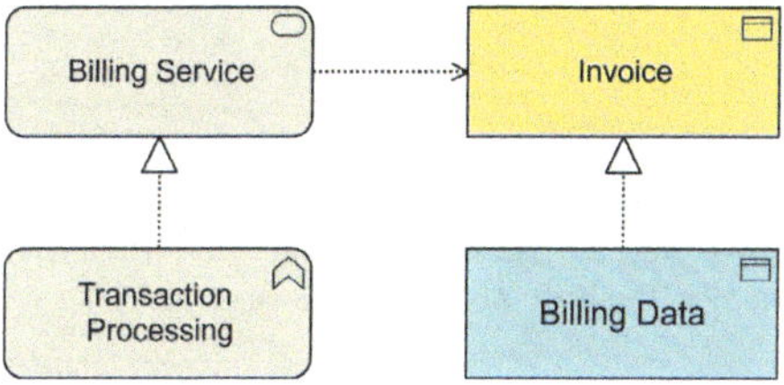

Example 4-4: Realization

4.2. Dependency Relationships

Dependency relationships describe how elements support or are used by other elements.

4.2.1. Serving Relationship

A serving relationship represents that an element provides its functionality to another element.

A serving relationship describes how the services or interfaces offered by a behavior or active structure element serve entities in their environment. This relationship is applied to both the behavior aspect and the active structure aspect.

Figure 4-6: Serving Notation

Example

Example 4-5 illustrates the serving relationship. The “Payment Interface” serves the “Customer”, while the “Payment Service” serves the “Pay Invoices” process of that customer.

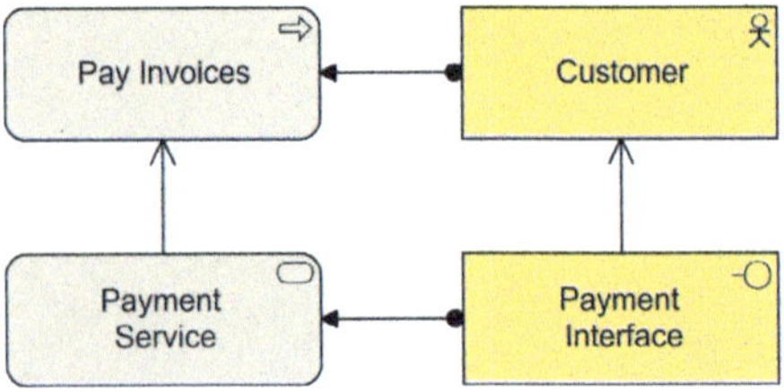

Example 4-5: Serving

4.2.2. Access Relationship

> An access relationship represents the ability of behavior and active structure elements to observe or act upon passive structure elements.

An access relationship indicates that a process, function, service, or event "does something" with a passive structure element; e.g., create, read, modify or delete a business or data object or an artifact; or produce, consume, move, transform, or destroy material. The relationship can also be used to indicate that the passive structure element . The relationship can also be used to indicate that the object is just associated with the behavior; e.g., it models the information that comes with an event, or the information that is made available as part of a service.

The arrowhead, if present, indicates the creation, change, or usage of passive structure elements.

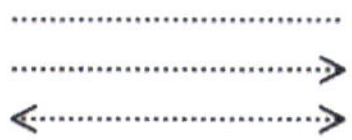

Figure 4-7: Access Notation

Example

> Example 4-6 illustrates the access relationship. The "Create Invoice" process writes/creates the "Invoice" business object; the "Send Invoice" process reads that object.

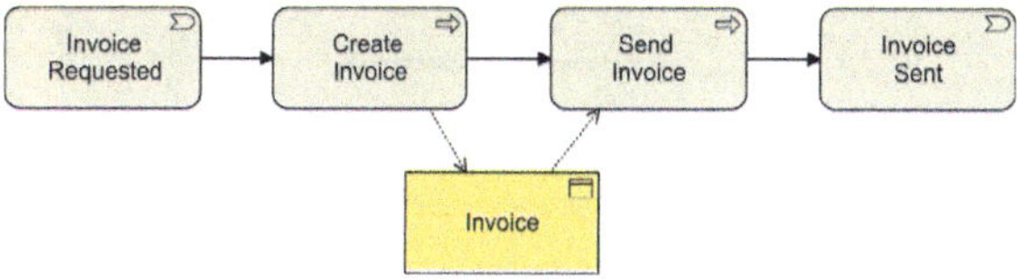

Example 4-6: Access

4.2.3. Influence Relationship

> An influence relationship represents that an element affects the implementation or achievement of some motivation element.

An influence relationship is used to describe some architectural elements that influence the achievement or implementation of a motivation element, such as a goal or a principle. In general, a motivation element is realized to a certain degree. For example, consistently satisfying the principle “serve customers wherever they are”, will help to make the goal “increase market share” come true. In other words, the principle contributes to the goal. In turn, to implement the principle “serve customers wherever they are”, it may be useful to impose a requirement of “24x7 web availability” on some customer-facing application component. This can be modeled as a requirement that has an influence on that principle and as an application component that in turn influences the requirement.

An influence relationship can be used to model either:

- The fact that an element positively contributes to the achievement or implementation of some motivation element
- The fact that an element negatively influences — i.e., prevents or counteracts — such achievement

Attributes can be used to indicate the sign and/or strength of the influence. The choice of possible attribute values is left to the modeler; e.g., {++, +, 0, -, --} or [0..10]. By default, the influence relationship models a contribution with unspecified sign and strength.

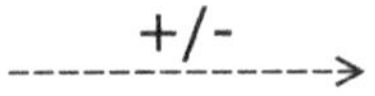

Figure 4-8: Influence Notation

Example

Example 4-7 illustrates the use of the influence relationship to model the different effects of the same requirement, "Assign Personal Assistant". This has a strongly positive influence on "Reduce Workload Of Employees", but a strongly negative influence on "Decrease Costs".

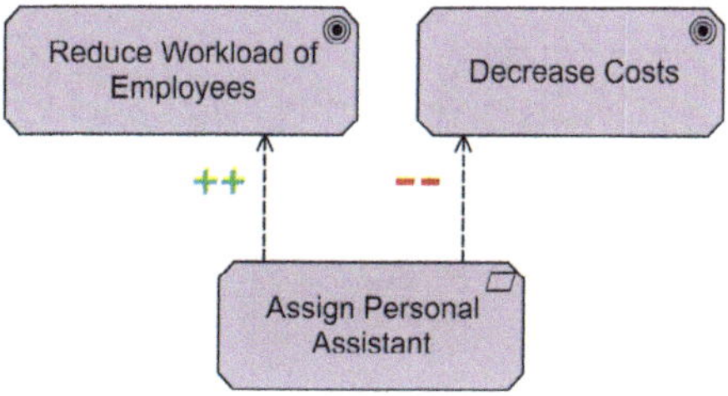

Example 4-7: Influence

4.2.4. Association Relationship

An association relationship represents an unspecified relationship, or one that is not represented by another ArchiMate relationship.

An association relationship is always allowed between two elements, or between a relationship and an element.

The association relationship can be used when drawing a first high-level model where relationships are initially denoted in a generic way, and later refined to show more specific relationship types.

Figure 4-9: Association Notation

Example

Example 4-8 illustrates two directed association relationships between a business object "Insurance Policy" and two business objects to which this business object refers. It also shows an association between a flow relationship and this "Insurance Policy", to indicate that the business object is transferred from "Policy Creation" to "Policy Management".

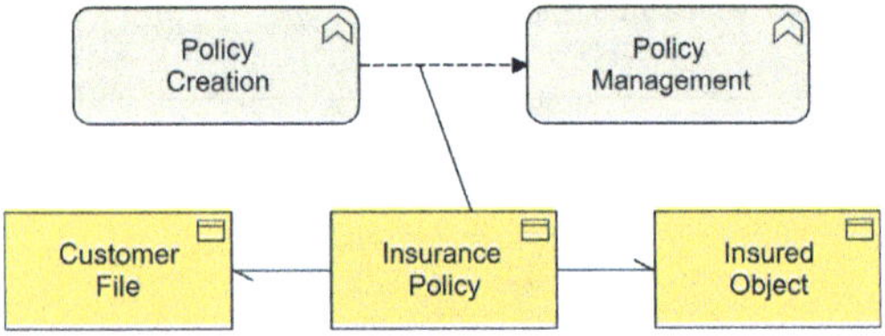

Example 4-8: Association

4.3. Dynamic Relationships

Dynamic relationships describe the architecture of a system "in motion".

4.3.1. Triggering Relationship

The triggering relationship represents a temporal or causal relationship between elements.

The triggering relationship is used to model the temporal or causal precedence of behavior elements in a process. The interpretation of a triggering relationship is that some part of the source element should be completed before the target element can start.

Figure 4-10: Triggering Notation

Example

Example 4-9 illustrates that triggering relationships are used to model causal dependencies between processes and/or events.

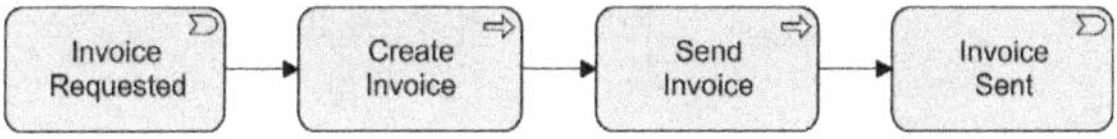

Example 4-9: Triggering

4.3.2. Flow Relationship

The flow relationship represents transfer from one element to another.

The flow relationship is used to model the flow of, for example, information, goods, or money between behavior elements. A flow relationship does not imply a causal relationship.

Figure 4-11: Flow Notation

Example

Example 4-10 shows a "Claim Assessment" function, which forwards decisions about the claims to the "Claim Settlement" function. In order to determine the order in which the claims should be assessed, "Claim Assessment" makes use of schedule information received from the "Scheduling" function.

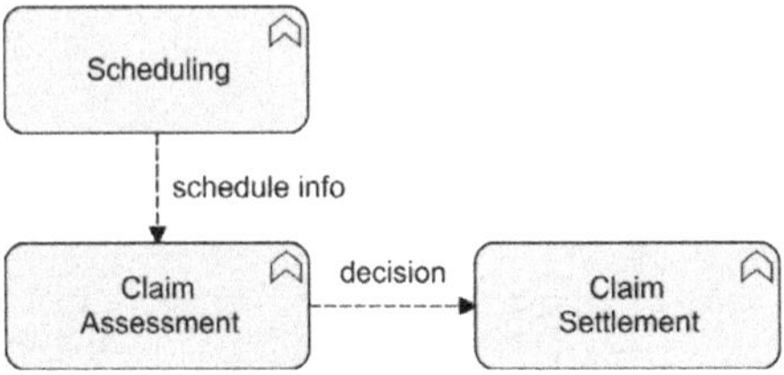

Example 4-10: Flow

4.4. Other Relationships

4.4.1. Specialization Relationship

The specialization relationship represents that an element is a particular kind of another element.

A specialization relationship is always allowed between two elements of the same type.

Figure 4-12: Specialization Notation

Example

Example 4-11 illustrates the use of the specialization relationship for a process. In this case, the "Take Out Travel Insurance" and "Take Out Luggage Insurance" processes are a specialization of a more generic "Take Out Insurance" process.

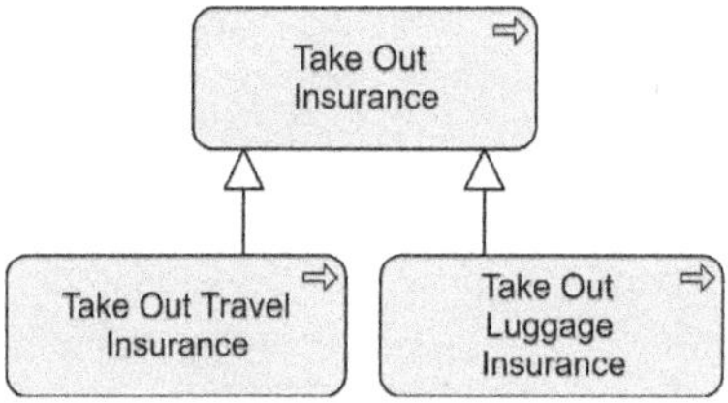

Example 4-11: Specialization

4.5. Junctions

4.5.1. Junction

A junction is not a relationship in the same sense as the other relationships described in this chapter, but rather a connector between relationships.

> A junction connects two or more relationships of the same type.

A junction may have multiple incoming relationships and one outgoing relationship, one incoming relationship and multiple outgoing relationships, or multiple incoming and outgoing relationships (the latter can be considered a shorthand of two contiguous junctions).

A junction is used to explicitly express that all elements together must participate in the relationship (and-junction) or that at least one of the elements participates in the relationship (or-junction). The or-junction can be used to express both inclusive and exclusive or conditions, which could be indicated by a modeler by naming the junction to reflect its type.

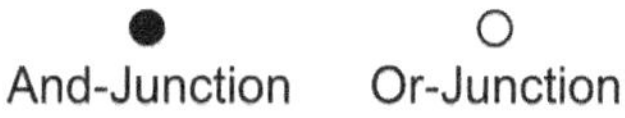

Figure 4-13: Junction Notation

Examples

In Example 4-12, the and-junction in the model is used to denote that the "Sales" and "Finance" functions together realize the "Invoicing" service.

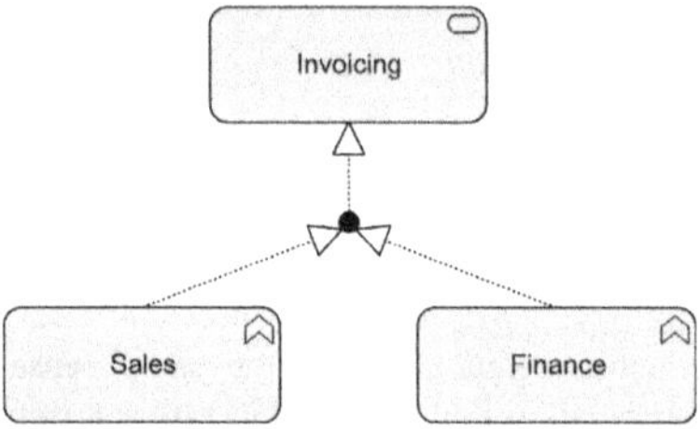

Example 4-12: And-Junction

In Example 4-13, the or-junction is used to denote a choice: process "Assess Request" triggers either "Accept Request" or "Reject Request". (The usual interpretation of two separate triggering relations, one from "Assess Request" to "Accept Request" and one from "Assess Request" to "Reject Request", is that "Assess Request" triggers both of the other processes.)

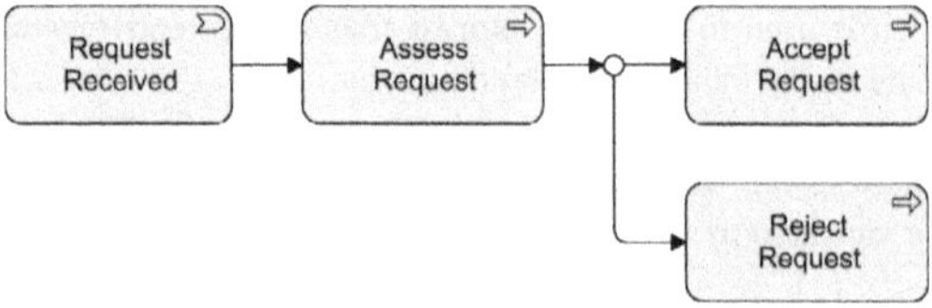

Example 4-13: Or-Junction

4.6. Multiplicity

All relationships can have on each end (except when connected to a junction) an attribute specifying how many instances are allowed at that end. The notation for this attribute can be:

- A single number *n* being a positive integer, meaning that exactly *n* instances are required on that end
- * (equivalent to 0..*), meaning that this end is unbounded
- *n..m* where *n* and *m* are non-negative integers and *m* is greater than *n*, meaning that any number of instances from *n* to *m* are allowed on that end

Using this notation, it is possible to indicate if the participation of an element in the relationship is optional (multiplicity on its end set to * or 0..m) or mandatory (multiplicity on its end set to n or n..m, with n being a positive integer).

Example

In Example 4-14, an "Insurance Policy" refers to at least one "Insured Object". A "Claim" is related to exactly one "Insurance Policy" and zero or more Claims may be related to that Insurance Policy.

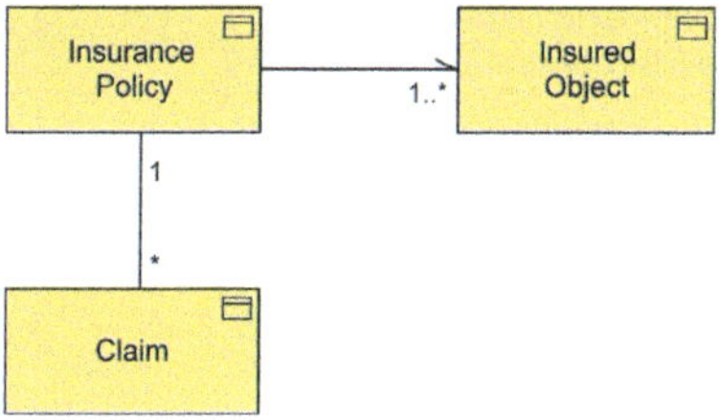

Example 4-14: Multiplicity

4.7. Summary

Table 4-1 provides a summary of the ArchiMate relationships and junctions with their definitions.

Table 4-1: Relationships and Junctions

Relationships	Definition	Notation	Role Names
Structural Relationships			
Aggregation	Represents that an element combines one or more other concepts.		→ aggregates ← aggregated in
Composition	Represents that an element combines one or more other concepts, where the existence of those concepts depends on that of the element.		→ composed of ← composed in
Assignment	Represents the allocation of responsibility, performance of behavior, storage, or execution.		→ assigned to ← has assigned
Realization	Represents that an element plays a critical role in the creation, achievement, sustenance, or operation of a more abstract element.	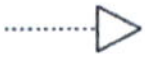	→ realizes ← realized by
Dependency Relationships			
Serving	Represents that an element provides its functionality to another element.		→ serves ← served by
Access	Represents the ability of behavior and active structure elements to observe or act upon passive structure elements.		→ accesses ← accessed by
Influence	Represents that an element affects the implementation or achievement of some motivation element.	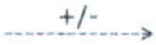	→ influences ← influenced by

Relationships	Definition	Notation	Role Names
Association	Represents an unspecified relationship, or one that is not represented by another ArchiMate relationship.		associated with → associated to ← associated from
Dynamic Relationships			
Triggering	Represents a temporal or causal relationship between elements.		→ triggers ← triggered by
Flow	Represents transfer from one element to another.		→ flows to ← flows from
Other Relationships			
Specialization	Represents that an element is a particular kind of another element.		→ specializes ← specialized by
Junctions			
Junction	Used to connect relationships of the same type.	 And-Junction  Or-Junction	

4.8. Derivation of Relationships

In the ArchiMate language, you can derive indirect relationships between elements in a model, based on the modeled relationships. This allows for the abstraction of irrelevant intermediary elements to present a specific model or view of the architecture that supports impact analysis.

The rules for making such derivations are defined in Appendix B of the standard.

Example

In Example 4-15, assume that the goal is to abstract from the functions, sub-functions, and services in the model. In this case, an indirect serving relationship (thick red arrow on the right) can be derived from "Financial Application" to the "Invoicing and Collections" process (from the chain assignment — aggregation — realization — serving).

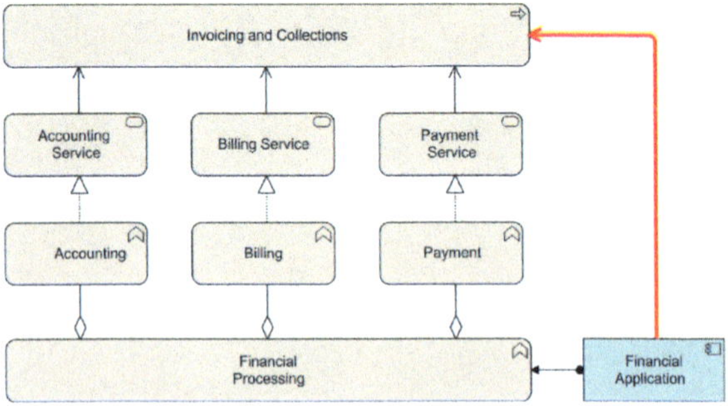

Example 4-15: Derivation from a Chain of Relationships

Derivation of relationships is intended as a way to create summaries of detailed models. It is a way to remove (to abstract from) details in a model while still making valid "statements". Hence, derivation is always meant to go from more detail to less detail. This mechanism is one of the unique properties of the ArchiMate language compared to other modeling languages.

The language allows the modeler to directly create relationships that are necessarily valid derived relationships without the constituents of the derivation being available in the model. These relationships (for example, a realization relationship between an application component and an application service) assume that the required constituents (for example, a function) needed for the derived relationship exist; however, these missing elements need not be modeled explicitly, and the derived relationships can be used as if they have not been derived. Thus, the modeler has full freedom in choosing the required level of detail.

Because the essence of derivation is to make simplifications or summaries, it cannot be used to infer more detail. Therefore, a realization relationship from an application component to an application service can be modeled, but from it, no conclusions can be drawn about the exact source of this derivation (e.g., which functions realize which services).

This is information that should be added by a modeler during the design process: a higher-level, more abstract model can be refined by elaborating the derived relationships (in the previous example by adding a function that realizes the application service and to which the application component is assigned).

It is important to note that all these derived relationships are also valid in the ArchiMate language. They are not shown in the metamodel diagrams included in the standard because this would reduce their legibility.

Chapter 5. Motivation Domain

Motivation elements are used to model the motivations, or reasons, that guide the design or change of an Enterprise Architecture.

> A motivation element represents the context of or reason behind the architecture of an enterprise.

5.1. Metamodel

Figure 5-1 gives an overview of the motivation elements and their relationships.

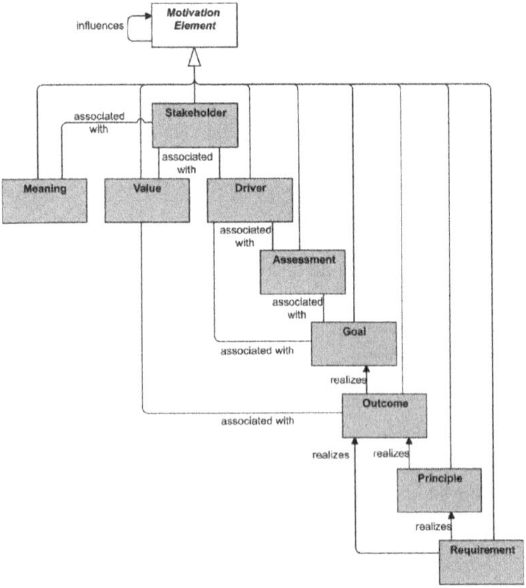

Figure 5-1: Motivation Elements Metamodel

5.2. Stakeholder, Driver, and Assessment

5.2.1. Stakeholder

A stakeholder represents the perspective from which a business actor perceives the effects of the architecture.

A stakeholder has one or more interests in, or concerns about, the organization and its Enterprise Architecture. In order to direct efforts to these interests and concerns, stakeholders change, set, and emphasize goals. Stakeholders may also influence each other. Examples of stakeholders are the Chief Executive Officer (CEO), the board of directors, shareholders, customers, business and application architects, but also legislative authorities. The name of a stakeholder should preferably be a noun.

Figure 5-2: Stakeholder Notation

5.2.2. Driver

A driver represents an external or internal condition that motivates an organization to define its goals and implement the changes necessary to achieve them.

Drivers that are associated with a stakeholder are often called "concerns" of that stakeholder. Drivers of change may be external to the enterprise (e.g., economic changes or changing legislation) and need not have a stakeholder associated with them. The name of a driver should preferably be a noun.

Figure 5-3: Driver Notation

5.2.3. Assessment

> An assessment represents the result of an analysis of the state of affairs of the enterprise with respect to some driver.

An assessment may reveal strengths, weaknesses, opportunities, or threats for some area of interest. These need to be addressed by adjusting existing goals or setting new ones, which may trigger changes to the Enterprise Architecture.

Strengths and weaknesses are internal to the organization. Opportunities and threats are external to the organization. Weaknesses and threats can be considered as problems that need to be addressed by goals that "negate" the weaknesses and threats. Strengths and opportunities may be translated directly into goals. For example, the weakness "Customers complain about the helpdesk" can be addressed by defining the goal "Improve helpdesk". Or the opportunity "Customers favor insurances that can be managed online" can be addressed by the goal "Introduce online portfolio management". The name of an assessment should preferably be a noun or a (very) short sentence.

Figure 5-4: Assessment Notation

5.2.4. Example

The stakeholder "Chief Marketing Officer (CMO)" is concerned with the driver "Market Share", the stakeholder "Chief Executive Officer (CEO)" is concerned with the drivers "Market Share" and "Profitability", and the stakeholder "Chief Financial Officer (CFO)" is concerned with the driver "Profitability". The driver "Profitability" consists of two other drivers: "Revenue" and "Costs". Several assessments are associated with these drivers (e.g., the assessment "Market Share Is Declining" is associated with driver "Market Share"), and assessments may influence each other in a positive or negative way (e.g., "Market Share Is Declining" results in "Revenue Is Declining", which in turn results in "Profitability Is Declining").

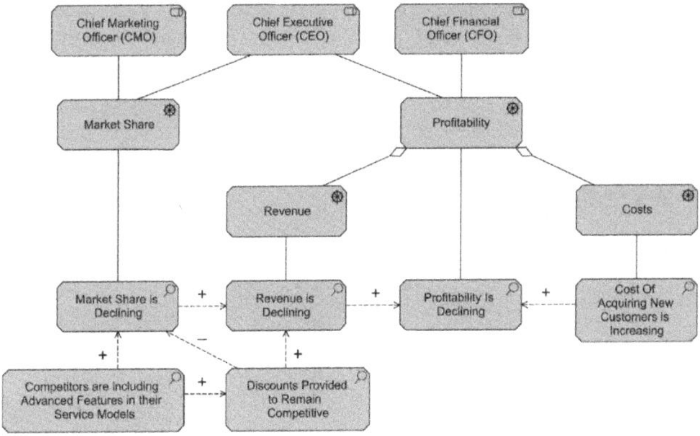

Example 5-1: Stakeholder, Driver, and Assessment

5.3. Goal, Outcome, Principle, and Requirement

5.3.1. Goal

> A goal represents a high-level statement of intent, direction, or desired end state for an organization and its stakeholders.

In principle, a goal can represent any objective a stakeholder may desire, such as a state of affairs, or a produced value. Examples of goals include: to increase profit, to reduce waiting times at the helpdesk, or to introduce online portfolio management. Goals are typically used to measure success of an organization.

Goals are generally expressed using qualitative words; e.g., "increase", "improve", or "easier". Goals can also be decomposed; e.g., "increase profit" can be decomposed into the goals "reduce cost" and "increase sales". However, it is also very common to associate concrete outcomes with goals, which can be used to describe both the quantitative and time-related results that are essential to describe the desired state, and when it should be achieved.

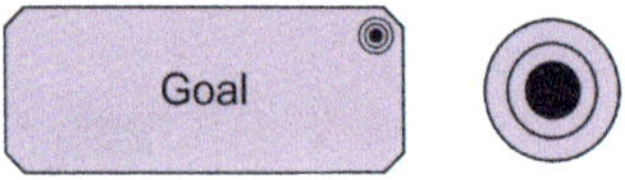

Figure 5-5: Goal Notation

5.3.2. Outcome

> An outcome represents an end result, effect, or consequence of a certain state of affairs.

Outcomes are high-level, business-oriented results produced by the capabilities of an organization and, by inference, by the core elements of its architecture that realize these capabilities. Outcomes are tangible, possibly quantitative, and time-related, and can be associated with assessments. An outcome may have a different value for different stakeholders.

Outcome names should unambiguously identify end results that have been achieved or are expected to be achieved at a definite point in the future. Examples include "First-place customer satisfaction ranking achieved" and "Key supplier partnerships in place". Outcome names can also be more specific; e.g., "10% year-over-year quarterly profits increase in 2018".

Figure 5-6: Outcome Notation

5.3.3. Principle

> A principle represents a statement of intent defining a general property that applies to any system in a certain context in the architecture.

Principles are strongly related to goals and requirements. Similar to requirements, principles define intended properties of systems. However, in contrast to requirements, principles are broader in scope and more abstract than requirements. For example, the principle "Information management processes comply with all relevant laws, policies, and regulations" is realized by the requirements that are imposed by the actual laws, policies, and regulations that apply to the specific system under design.

Figure 5-7: Principle Notation

5.3.4. Requirement

> A requirement represents a statement of need defining a property that applies to a specific system as described by the architecture.

Requirements model the properties of these elements that are needed to achieve the “ends” that are modeled by the goals. In this respect, requirements represent the “means” to realize goals.

During the design process, goals may be decomposed until the resulting sub-goals are sufficiently detailed to enable their realization by properties that can be exhibited by systems. At this point, goals can be realized by requirements that demand these properties from the systems.

For example, two alternative requirements may be identified to realize the goal “Improve portfolio management”:

- By assigning a personal assistant to each customer
- By introducing online portfolio management

The first requirement can be realized by a human actor and the second by a software application. These requirements can be decomposed further to define the requirements on the human actor and the software application in more detail.

Figure 5-8: Requirement Notation

5.3.5. Example

The goal “Improve Profitability of Service Offering” is realized by the outcome “Increased Profit by 10% in Next Fiscal Year”. This outcome is influenced positively by the outcomes “Increased Revenue by 20% in Next Fiscal Year” and “Reduced Cost of Customer Acquisition by 25%”. The outcome “Increased Revenue by 20% in Next Fiscal Year” is influenced positively by an outcome “Increased Market Share by 10% in Next Fiscal Year”. There is also a negative outcome: “Increased Technology Expenditure by 10%”. These outcomes are realized by a combination of two principles: “Serve Customers Wherever They Are” and “Serve Customers Whenever They Need Our Help”. Both of these principles are realized by a combination of two requirements: “Mobile Applications Shall Run On All Popular Mobile Platforms” and “Services Shall Be Accessible Through Mobile Browsers”. The outcome “Reduced Cost Of Customer Acquisition by 25%” is realized by a principle “Respond To Changing Customer Needs, Preferences, and Expectations Quickly and Efficiently”, which in turn is realized by a requirement “Mobile Applications Shall Be Built With Cross-Platform Frameworks”.

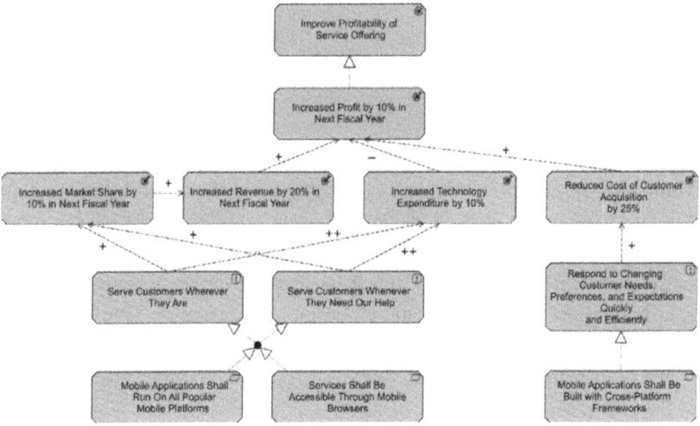

Example 5-2: Goal, Outcome, Principle, and Requirement

5.4. Meaning and Value

5.4.1. Meaning

Meaning represents the knowledge or expertise present in, or the interpretation given to, a concept in a particular context.

A meaning represents the interpretation of a concept of the architecture. In particular, this is used to describe the meaning of passive structure elements (for example, a document, a message). It is a description that expresses the *intent* of that element; i.e., how it informs the *external user*.

A meaning can be associated with any concept. To denote that a meaning is specific to a particular stakeholder, this stakeholder can also be associated to the meaning. The name of a meaning should preferably be a noun or noun phrase.

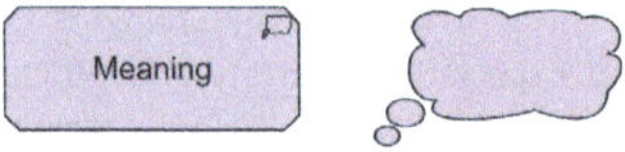

Figure 5-9: Meaning Notation

5.4.2. Value

Value represents the relative worth, utility, or importance of a concept.

Value represents the usefulness, advantage, benefit, desirability, or gain for a customer, stakeholder, or end user by, for example, selling a product, using a service, or completing some activity. Value is often expressed in terms of money, but it has long since been recognized that non-monetary value is also essential to business; for example, practical/functional value (including the *right* to use a service), and the value of information or knowledge.

Value may also be negative. For instance, the introduction of an Artificial Intelligence (AI) chatbot on a company website may have a positive value (efficiency) for that company but a negative value (frustration) for customers.

A value can be associated with any concept. To model the stakeholder for whom this value applies, this stakeholder can also be associated with that value. Although the name of a value can be expressed in many different ways (including amounts, objects), where the "functional" value of an architecture element is concerned, it is recommended to try and express it as an action or state that can be performed or reached as a result of the corresponding element being available.

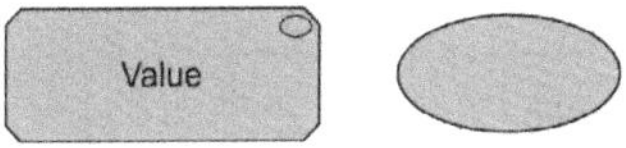

Figure 5-10: Value Notation

5.4.3. Example

Sending a "Push Notification" has a value of "Cost Efficiency" for the stakeholder "Insurer", and a value and "Peace of Mind" (which is partly due to a value of "Certainty") for the stakeholder "Customer". Different meanings can be assigned to the different specific types of notification messages. A "Confirmation Of Receipt Message" has the meaning "The Insurer has acknowledged and registered a claim", a "Review Complete Message" has the meaning "Claim review has been completed, so the Customer can expect a decision soon", and a "Payment Complete Message" has the meaning "Payment has been authorized and funds have been transferred to the Customer nominated account".

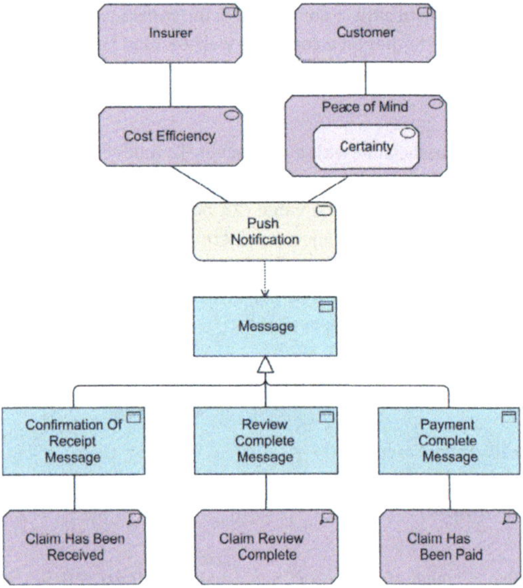

Example 5-3: Meaning and Value

5.5. Summary

Table 5-1 provides a summary of the motivation elements, with their definitions.

Table 5-1: Motivation Elements

Element	Definition	Notation
Stakeholder	The perspective from which a business actor perceives the effects of the architecture.	
Driver	An external or internal condition that motivates an organization to define its goals and implement the changes necessary to achieve them.	
Assessment	The result of an analysis of the state of affairs of the enterprise with respect to some driver.	
Goal	A high-level statement of intent, direction, or desired end state for an organization and its stakeholders.	
Outcome	An end result, effect, or consequence of a certain state of affairs.	
Principle	A statement of intent defining a general property that applies to any system in a certain context in the architecture.	
Requirement	A statement of need defining a property that applies to a specific system as described by the architecture.	
Meaning	The knowledge or expertise present in, or the interpretation given to, a concept in a particular context.	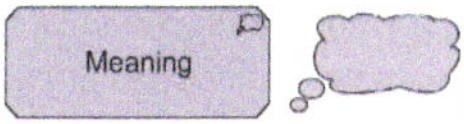
Value	The relative worth, utility, or importance of a concept.	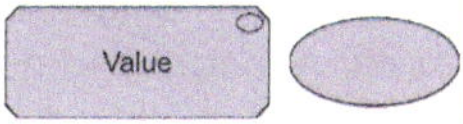

Chapter 6. Strategy Domain

The strategy elements are typically used to model the strategic direction and choices of an enterprise, as far as the impact on its architecture is concerned.

6.1. Metamodel

Figure 6-1 gives an overview of the strategy elements and their relationships.

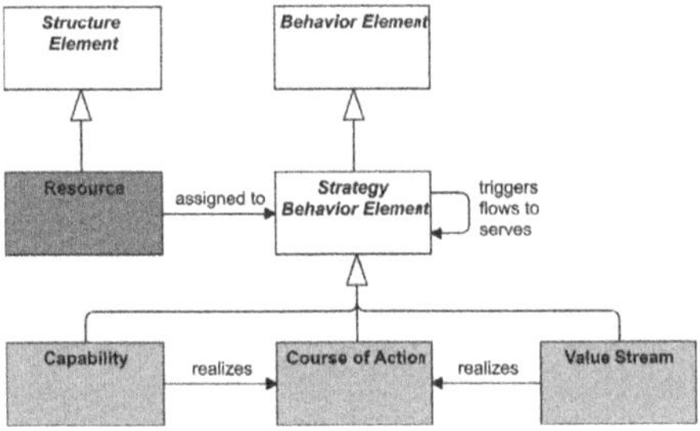

Figure 6-1: Strategy Elements Metamodel

6.2. Structure Elements

6.2.1. Resource

A resource represents a useful or valuable possession or means that can be drawn upon by the enterprise.

Resources are a central concept in the field of strategic management, economics, computer science, portfolio management, and more. They are often recognized along with capabilities, to be sources of competitive advantage for organizations.

Resources can be classified in different ways, including tangible assets, intangible assets, and human assets. Examples of tangible assets include financial assets (cash, securities, borrowing capacity, etc.) and physical assets (plant, equipment, land, mineral reserves, etc.). Examples of intangible assets include technology assets (patents, copyrights, trade secrets, etc.), reputation assets (brand, relationships, etc.), and culture assets. Examples of human assets include skills/know-how, capacity for communication and collaboration, and motivation.

The name of a resource should preferably be a noun.

Figure 6-2: Resource Notation

6.3. Behavior Elements

6.3.1. Capability

> A capability represents an ability that an organizational entity, person, or system possesses.

Capabilities are classified as behavior in the ArchiMate language because they describe abilities: what the enterprise can (is able to) *do* (now or in the future). Capabilities are expressed in general, high-level terms that are typically realized by a combination of organization, people, processes, information, and technology. For example, business planning, customer management, or asset management.

Capabilities are typically aimed at achieving some outcome. Capabilities are themselves realized by core behavior elements. To denote that a set of core elements together realizes a capability, grouping can be used.

Capabilities are often used for capability-based planning, to describe their evolution over time. To model such so-called capability increments, the specialization relationship can be used to denote that a certain capability increment is a specific version of that capability. Aggregating those increments and the core elements that realize them in plateaus (see Section 11.2.3) can be used to model the evolution of the capabilities.

The name of a capability should emphasize "what we do" rather than "how we do it". Typically, it should be expressed as a compound noun or gerund (-ing form of verb); e.g., "Risk Management", "Market Development", "Product Engineering", etc.

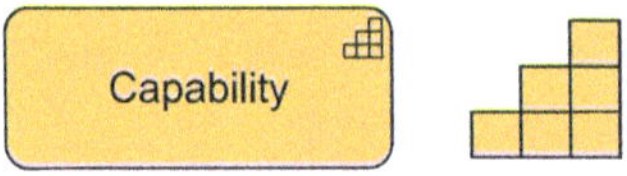

Figure 6-3: Capability Notation

6.3.2. Value Stream

A value stream represents a sequence of activities that create an overall result for a customer, stakeholder, or end user.

A value stream describes how an enterprise organizes its activities to create value.

Value streams may be defined at different levels of the organization; e.g., at the enterprise level, business unit level, or department level. Value streams can be an aggregation of value-adding activities. These are also modeled with the value stream element and known as value (stream) stages, each of which creates and adds incremental value from one stage to the next. These stages are typically related using flow relationships to model the flow of value between them. Resources can be assigned to value streams and capabilities can serve (i.e., enable) a value stream.

Value streams are typically realized by processes and possibly other core behavior elements. The stages in a value stream provide a framework for organizing and defining processes, but different parts of the organization may have their own implementations of processes that realize the same value stream stage.

It is recommended that the name of a value stream be expressed using a verb-noun construct in the active tense; e.g., "Acquire Insurance Product".

Figure 6-4: Value Stream Notation

6.3.3. Course of Action

A course of action represents an approach or plan for configuring some capabilities and resources of the enterprise, to achieve a goal.

A course of action represents what an enterprise has decided to do to achieve its objectives. Courses of action can be categorized as strategies and tactics. It is not possible to make a hard distinction between the two, but strategies tend to be long term and fairly broad in scope, while tactics tend to be short term and narrower in scope.

Figure 6-5: Course of Action Notation

6.4. Examples

"Increase Profit" is a goal that consists of other goals: "Decrease Costs" and "Increase Revenues". The former is related to the "Operational Excellence" strategy of the company, modeled as a course of action. This is decomposed into two other courses of action: "Centralize IT Systems" and "Standardize Products". These result in two outcomes: "Decreased Costs" and "Loss of Customers", which influence the goals in positive and negative ways. This shows an important difference between goals and outcomes: not all outcomes lead to the intended results.

The courses of action are realized by a number of capabilities: "IT Management & Operations" and "Product Management", and appropriate resources "Human Resources" and "IT Resources" are assigned to the former. The model fragment also shows that these resources are located in the "Headquarters" of the organization, in line with the "Centralize IT Systems" course of action.

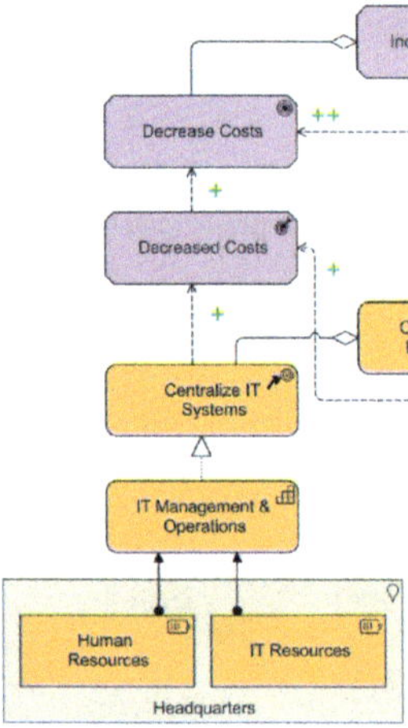

Example 6-1: Capability, Resource, and Course of Action

Example 6-2 shows a model of a high-level value stream for an insurance company, where each stage in the value stream is served by a number of capabilities. Between these stages, we see the value flows, and each stage realizes a specific value item (modeled as an outcome), which has a specific value. Together, these outcomes comprise the overall outcome that this value stream realizes for a stakeholder, the customer.

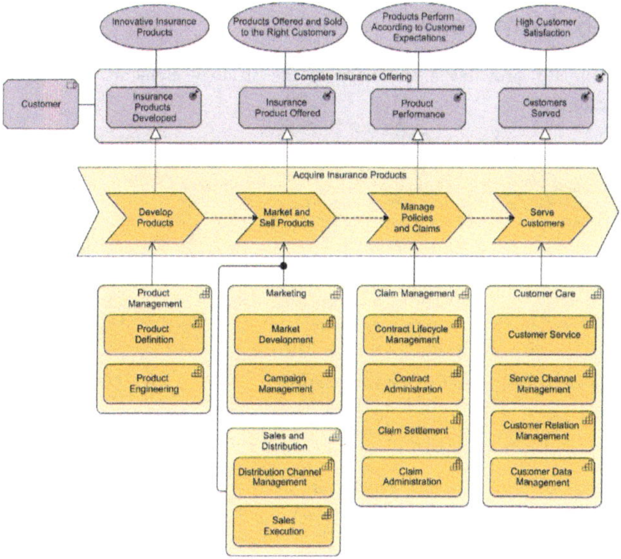

Example 6-2: Value Stream with Capability Cross-Mapping

6.5. Summary

Table 6-1 provides a summary of the strategy elements, with their definitions.

Table 6-1: Strategy Elements

Element	Description	Notation
Resource	A useful or valuable possession or means that can be drawn upon by the enterprise.	
Capability	An ability that an organizational entity, person, or system, possesses.	
Value Stream	A sequence of activities that create an overall result for a customer, stakeholder, or end user.	
Course of Action	An approach or plan for configuring some capabilities and resources of the enterprise, to achieve a goal.	

Chapter 7. Business Domain

Business Domain elements are used to model the operational organization of an enterprise in a technology-independent manner, whereas strategy elements (see Chapter 6) are used to model the strategic direction and choices of the enterprise.

7.1. Metamodel

Figure 7-1 gives an overview of the active and passive structure elements in the Business Domain and their relationships. "Internal Active Structure Element", "External Active Structure Element", and "Passive Structure Element" are abstract elements; only their specializations (as defined in the following sections) are instantiated in models.

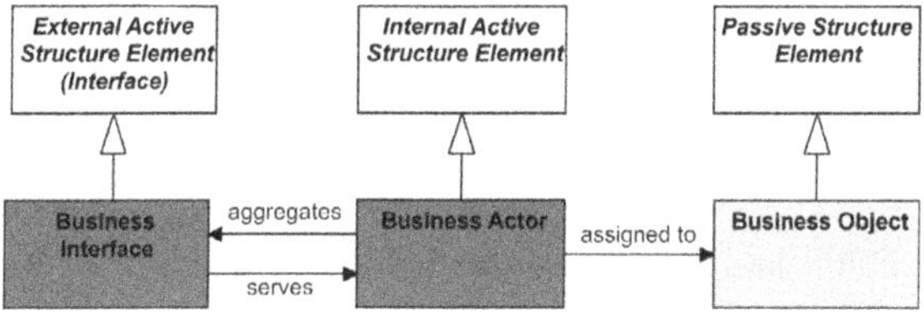

Figure 7-1: Business Structure Metamodel

7.2. Active Structure Elements

7.2.1. Business Actor

> A business actor represents a business entity that is capable of performing behavior.

A business actor is a business entity as opposed to a technical entity; i.e., it belongs to the Business Domain. Actors may, however, include entities outside the actual organization; e.g., customers and partners.

A business actor may be assigned to one or more roles. It can then perform the behavior to which these roles are assigned. Business actors can also be assigned to business objects, to express that someone is responsible for some specific information or another kind of business object.

The name of a business actor should preferably be a noun. Business actors may be specific individuals or organizations; e.g., "John Smith" or "ABC Corporation", or they may be generic; e.g., "customer" or "supplier".

Figure 7-2: Business Actor Notation

7.2.2. Business Interface

A business interface represents a point of access where a business actor makes services available to its environment.

A business interface exposes the functionality of a service that is provided by a business actor. It is often referred to as a channel (telephone, Internet, local office, etc.). The same service may be exposed through different interfaces.

A business interface may be part of a business actor through an aggregation relationship, and a business interface may serve a role or business actor. A business interface may be assigned to one or more services, which means that these services are exposed by the interface. The name of a business interface should preferably be a noun.

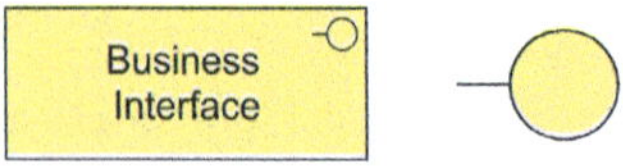

Figure 7-3: Business Interface Notation

7.2.3. Example

The "ArchiSurance Back Office", modeled as a business actor, consists of the "Travel Department", "Home Department", and "Legal Department". Respectively, these are assigned to the roles "Travel Insurance Claims Assessor", "Home Insurance Claims Assessor", and "Senior Claims Specialist". Moreover, the "ArchiSurance Back Office" has four different business interfaces that serve the "Customer" business actor.

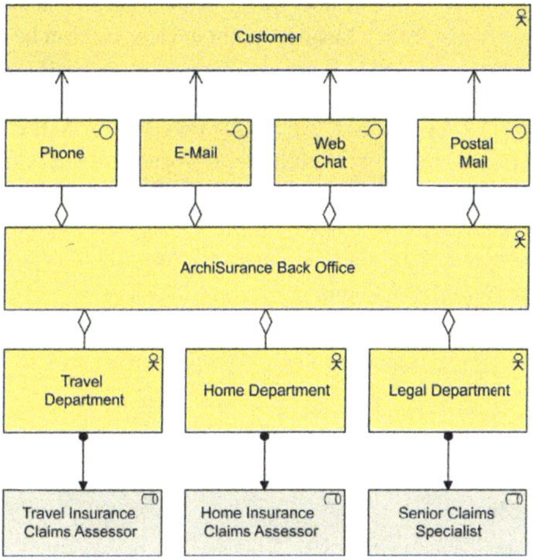

Example 7-1: Business Active Structure Elements

7.3. Passive Structure Elements

7.3.1. Business Object

A business object represents a conceptual passive element that has relevance from a business perspective.

A wide variety of types of business objects can be defined. Business objects are passive in the sense that they do not trigger or perform processes. A business object could be used to represent information assets that are relevant from a business point of view and can be realized by data objects.

Business objects may be accessed (e.g., in the case of information objects, they may be created, read, or written) by a process, function, event, or service. A business object may have association, specialization, or aggregation relationships with other business objects. A business object may be realized by a data object or material. The name of a business object should preferably be a noun.

Figure 7-4: Business Object Notation

7.3.2. Example

The example shows that an "Insurance Policy" refers to one or more "Insured Objects". An "Insurance Policy" can have zero or more "Claims" filed against it, and each "Claim" must refer to exactly one "Insurance Policy".

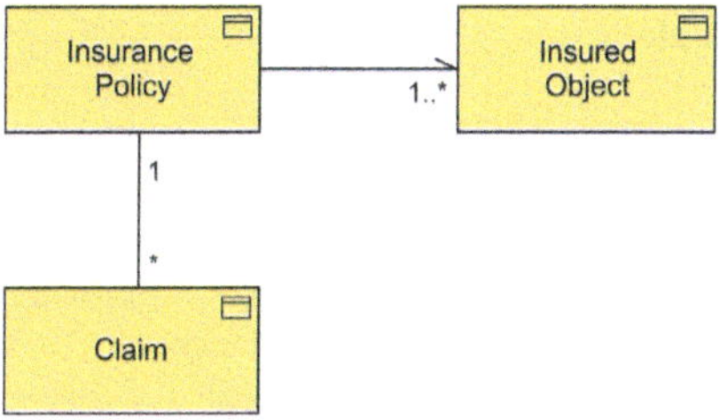

Example 7-2: Business Passive Structure Elements

7.4. Composite Elements

7.4.1. Product

A product represents a coherent collection of services, business objects, data objects, artifacts, and/or material, which is offered as a whole to (internal or external) customers.

This definition covers both intangible, services-based, or information products that are common in information-intensive organizations, as well as tangible, physical products.

A product may aggregate services, business objects, data objects, artifacts, and material. Hence a product may aggregate elements from domains other than the Business Domain.

A value may be associated with a product. The name of a product is usually the name used in the communication with customers, or possibly a more generic noun (e.g., "Travel Insurance").

Figure 7-5: Product Notation

7.4.2. Example

A product "Insurance" consists of a business object "Insurance Policy" and a service "Customer Service", which aggregates four other services: "Application", "Renewal", "Claims Processing", and "Appeal". An "Auto Insurance" product is a specialization of the generic "Insurance" product, with an additional service "Drive Well and Save", and accompanying "Drive Well and Save Agreement" modeled as a business object.

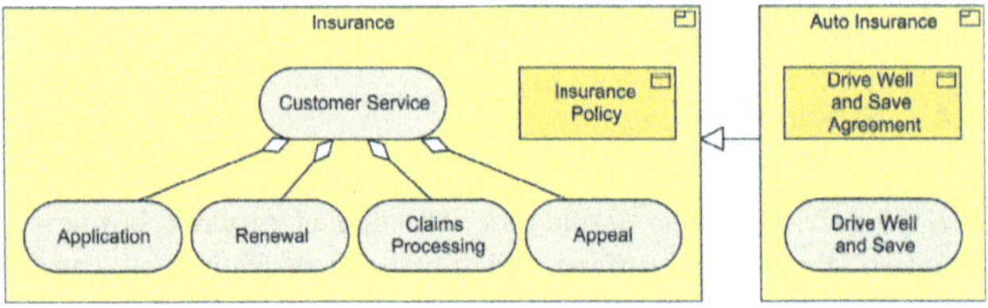

Example 7-3: Business Composite Element: Product

7.5. Summary

Table 7-1 provides a summary of the Business Domain elements, with their definitions.

Table 7-1: Business Domain Elements

Element	Description	Notation
Business Actor	A business entity that is capable of performing behavior.	
Business Interface	A point of access where a business actor makes services available to its environment.	
Business Object	A passive element that has relevance from a business perspective.	
Product	A coherent collection of services, business objects, data objects, artifacts and/or material, which is offered as a whole to (internal or external) customers.	

Chapter 8. Application Domain

The Application Domain elements are typically used to model the Application Architecture that describes the structure, behavior, and interaction of the applications of the enterprise.

8.1. Metamodel

Figure 8-1 gives an overview of the active and passive structure elements in the Application Domain and their relationships.

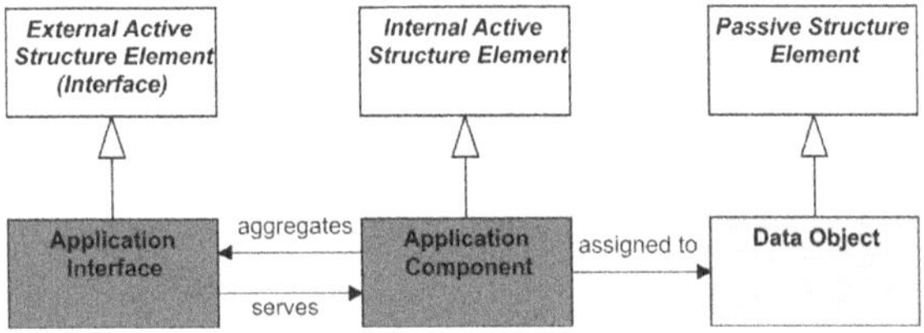

Figure 8-1: Application Structure Metamodel

8.2. Active Structure Elements

8.2.1. Application Component

> An application component represents an encapsulation of application functionality aligned to implementation structure, which is modular and replaceable.

An application component is a self-contained unit. As such, it is independently deployable, re-usable, and replaceable. It encapsulates its behavior and data, exposes services, and makes them available through interfaces. The name of an application component should preferably be a noun.

The application component element is used to model entire applications, and individual parts of such applications, at all relevant levels of detail.

Figure 8-2: Application Component Notation

8.2.2. Application Interface

An application interface represents a point of access where an application component makes its services available to its environment.

An application interface specifies how the functionality of a component can be accessed by other elements. An application interface exposes services of an application component to the environment. The same service may be exposed through different interfaces and the same interface may expose multiple services.

An application interface may be part of an application component through aggregation, which means that this interface is provided by that component and can serve other application components. An application interface can be assigned to services, which means that the interface exposes these services to the environment. The name of an application interface should preferably be a noun.

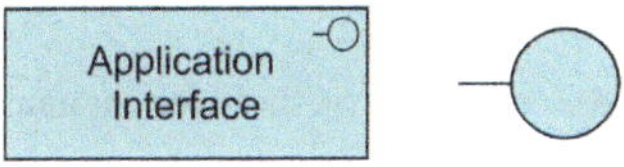

Figure 8-3: Application Interface Notation

8.2.3. Example

The "Online Travel Insurance Sales" collaboration aggregates two application components: "Quotation" and "Purchase". The collaboration provides an application interface "Web Services Interface" that serves another application component "Travel Website".

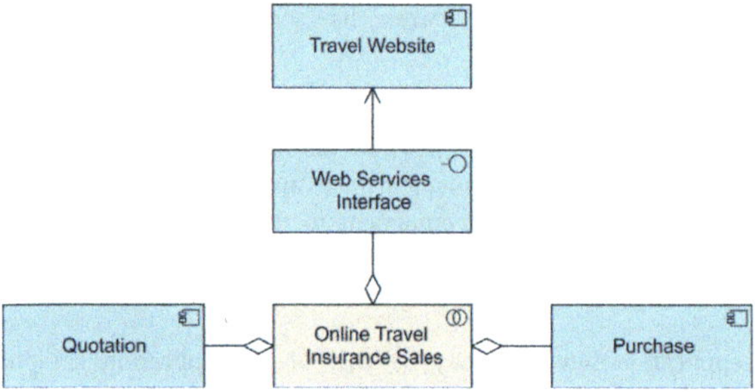

Example 8-1: Application Active Structure Elements

8.3. Passive Structure Elements

8.3.1. Data Object

A data object represents data structured for automated processing.

A data object should be a self-contained piece of information with a clear meaning to the business, not just to the application level. Typical examples of data objects are a customer record, a client data set, or an insurance claim.

The name of a data object should preferably be a noun.

Figure 8-4: Data Object Notation

8.3.2. Example

An "Online Insurance Quotation" data object aggregates three other data objects: "Quoted Price", "Terms and Conditions", and "Certificate of Authenticity". "Auto Insurance Quotation" and "Travel Insurance Quotation" are two specializations of the "Online Insurance Quotation" data object. "Travel Insurance Quotation" contains an additional data object "Purchased Itinerary".

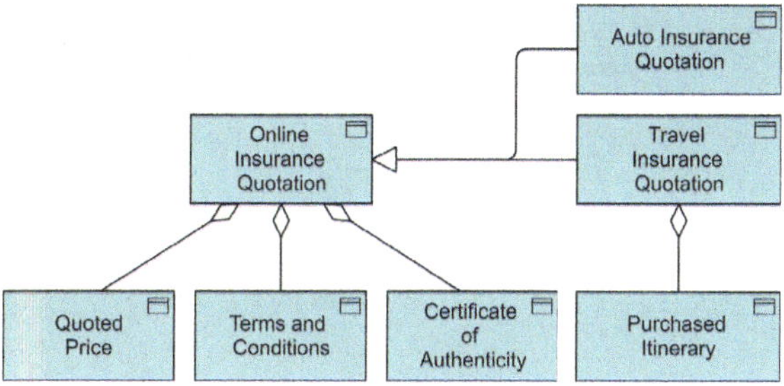

Example 8-2: Application Passive Structure Elements

8.4. Summary

Table 8-1 provides a summary of the Application Domain elements, with their definitions.

Table 8-1: Application Domain Elements

Element	Definition	Notation
Application Component	An encapsulation of application functionality aligned to implementation structure, which is modular and replaceable.	
Application Interface	A point of access where an application component makes services available to its environment.	
Data Object	Data structured for automated processing.	

Chapter 9. Technology Domain

The Technology Domain elements are typically used to model the Technology Architecture of the enterprise, describing the structure and behavior of the technology infrastructure of the enterprise. This comprises both information technology and operational/physical technology, and combinations thereof.

9.1. Metamodel

Figure 9-1 gives an overview of Active Structure Elements in the Technology Domain.

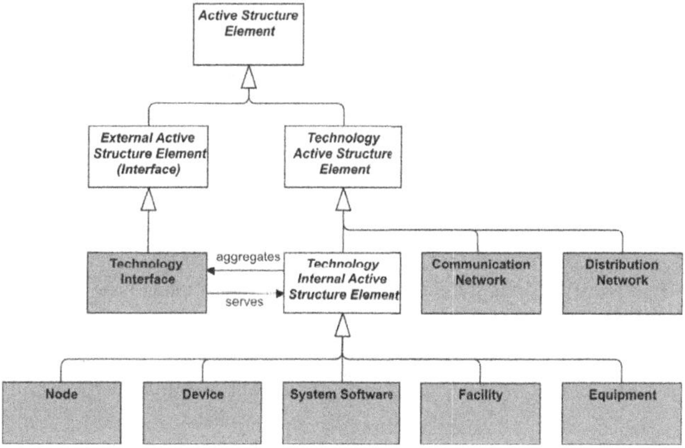

Figure 9-1: Technology Active Structure Elements

Figure 9-2 shows the relationships of the Technology Active Structure Elements.

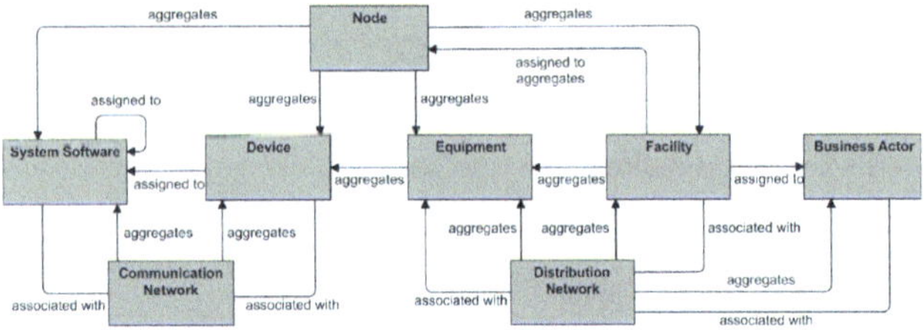

Figure 9-2: Technology Active Structure Relationships

9.2. Active Structure Elements

9.2.1. Node

A node represents a generic IT or physical structure that hosts, manipulates, or interacts with other such structures.

Nodes are active structure elements that perform behavior and execute, store, and process artifacts or materials. For instance, nodes are used to model application platforms.

The name of a node should preferably be a noun. A node may consist of sub-nodes.

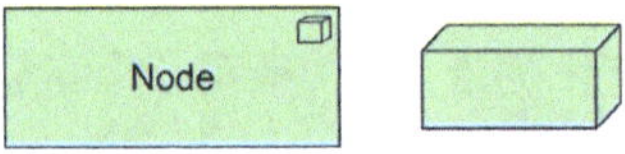

Figure 9-3: Node Notation

9.2.2. Technology Interface

A technology interface represents a point of access where a node, device, system software, facility, or equipment makes services available to its environment.

A technology interface specifies how the services of a technology internal active structure element can be accessed by other elements. A technology interface exposes a service to the environment. The same service may be exposed through different interfaces.

The name of a technology interface should preferably be a noun.

Figure 9-4: Technology Interface Notation

9.2.3. Device

A device represents IT hardware (possibly virtualized) used for processing, data storage, and similar purposes.

A device represents an IT resource with processing capability. It is typically used to model hardware systems such as mainframes, PCs, smartphones, or routers. It can also be used to model virtualized hardware; e.g., in an Infrastructure as a Service (IaaS) environment. Usually, devices are part of a node together with system software. Devices may be composite; i.e., aggregate sub-devices.

The name of a device should preferably be a noun phrase referring to the type of hardware (e.g., "IBM® Z Mainframe") or its usage (e.g., "Application Server").

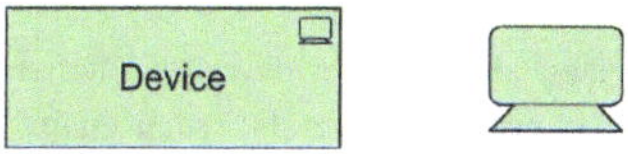

Figure 9-5: Device Notation

9.2.4. System Software

System software represents software that provides or contributes to an environment for storing, executing, and using software or data deployed within it.

System software is used to model the software environment in which artifacts run. This can be an operating system, a Java®, Enterprise Edition (JEE) application server, a database system, or a workflow engine. System software can also be used to represent communication middleware.

The name of system software should preferably be a noun referring to the type of execution environment; e.g., "JEE server". System software may aggregate other system software; e.g., an operating system containing a database.

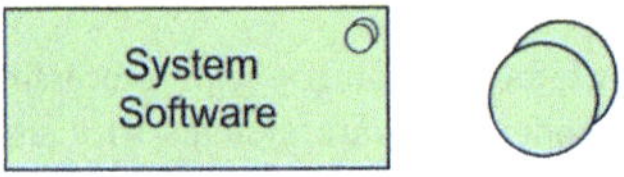

Figure 9-6: System Software Notation

9.2.5. Equipment

Equipment represents a physical machine, tool, instrument, or livestock.

Equipment comprises all active processing elements that carry out physical processes in which materials are used or transformed. It is possible to model nodes that are formed by a combination of IT infrastructure (devices, system software) and physical infrastructure (equipment); e.g., a Magnetic Resonance Imaging (MRI) scanner at a hospital, a production plant with its control systems, etc.

The name of a piece of equipment should preferably be a noun.

Figure 9-7: Equipment Notation

9.2.6. Facility

A facility represents a physical structure or environment.

A facility represents a physical resource that has the capability of facilitating (e.g., housing or locating) the use of equipment. It is typically used to model factories, buildings, or outdoor constructions that have an important role in production or distribution processes, and also IT-related facilities. Examples of facilities include a factory, laboratory, warehouse, shopping mall, cave, data center, or spaceship.

The name of a facility should preferably be a noun referring to the type of facility; e.g., "Rotterdam oil refinery".

Figure 9-8: Facility Notation

9.2.7. Communication Network

A communication network represents a set of IT structures for transmission, routing, and reception of data.

A communication network represents the physical communication infrastructure.

The most basic communication network is a single link between two devices, but it may comprise multiple links and required network equipment or software. A network has properties such as bandwidth and latency.

A communication network can consist of sub-networks. It can aggregate devices and system software to model the routers, switches, and firewalls that are part of the network infrastructure.

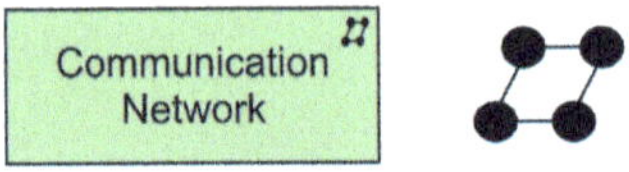

Figure 9-9: Communication Network Notation

9.2.8. Distribution Network

> A distribution network represents a physical network used to transport materials or energy.

A distribution network represents the physical distribution or transportation infrastructure. It embodies the physical realization of the logical paths between facilities.

A distribution network can be associated with the facilities it connects, and may realize one or more paths. A distribution network can consist of sub-networks and can aggregate facilities and equipment to model, for example, railway stations and trains that are part of a rail network.

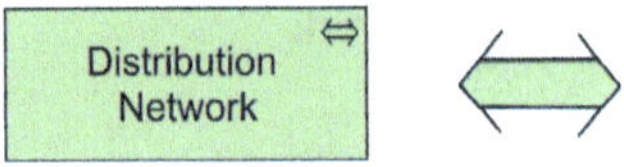

Figure 9-10: Distribution Network Notation

9.3. Passive Structure Elements

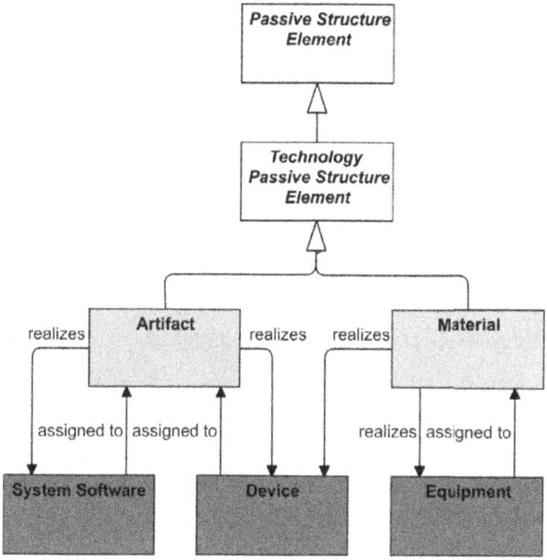

Figure 9-11: Technology Passive Structure Elements

9.3.1. Artifact

> An artifact represents a piece of data that is used or produced in a software development process, or by deployment and operation of an IT system.

An artifact represents a "physical" element in the IT world. Artifact is a specialization of technology passive structure elements. It is typically used to model (software) products such as source files, executables, scripts, database tables, messages, documents, specifications, and model files. It can be accessed (created, deleted, read, written) by behavior elements. An instance (copy) of an artifact can be deployed on a device or system software; this is modeled with an assignment relationship. An artifact could be used to represent a physical data component that realizes a data object.

The name of an artifact should preferably be the kind of artifact or the name of the file it represents; e.g., “virtual image”, “monitoring script”, or “order.jar”. An artifact may consist of sub-artifacts.

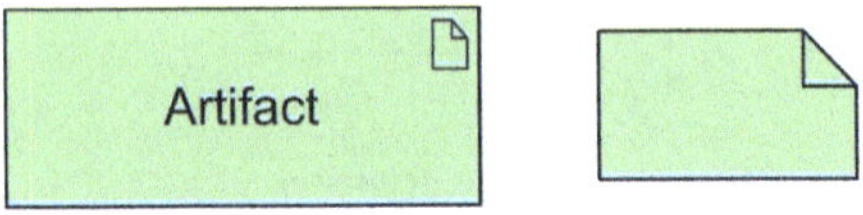

Figure 9-12: Artifact Notation

9.3.2. Material

Material represents tangible physical matter or energy.

Material is typically used to model raw materials and physical products, and also energy sources such as fuel and electricity. Material can be accessed by behavior elements to model how it is created, used, moved, transformed, or otherwise manipulated. Equipment may be assigned to material, to model where the material is stored.

This allows a distinction to be modeled between, for instance, “the sand is in the dump truck” and “the sand is poured into the concrete mixer”. Material may realize equipment.

The name of material should be a noun. Pieces of material may aggregate other pieces of material.

Figure 9-13: Material Notation

9.4. Example

The example shows a "Patient" and "Doctor", where the "Patient (Body)" (modeled as material) is scanned by an "MRI Scanner" that is part of "Medical Imaging" at the "Hospital. The "Raw Image Data" coming out of this scanner is transferred to the "Image Processing Server", on which the "Image Processing Software" runs. The resulting "Image Files" are read by the "Image Analysis Application" that the "Doctor" uses to provide a "Diagnosis" to the "Patient".

A more elaborate view could also show, for instance, how a Communication Network is used to transfer image data, or how a Distribution Network transports patients around the hospital. For the sake of clarity, these details have been left out here.

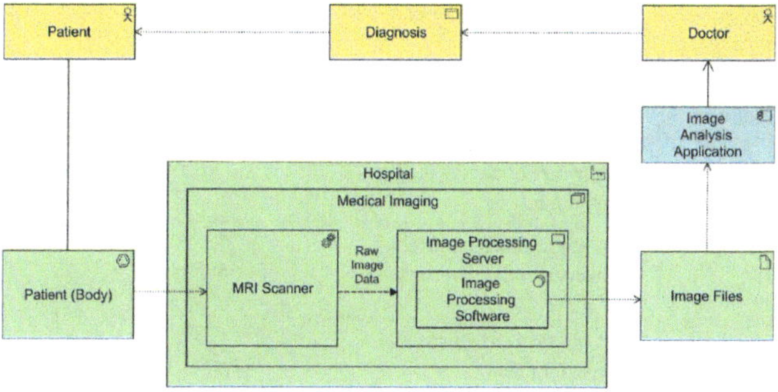

Example 9-1: Technology Elements

9.5. Summary

Table 9-1 provides a summary of the Technology Domain elements, with their definitions.

Table 9-1: Technology Domain Elements

Element	Definition	Notation
Node	A generic IT or physical structure that hosts, manipulates, or interacts with other such structures.	
Technology Interface	A point of access where a node, device, system software, facility, or equipment makes services available to its environment.	
Device	IT hardware (possibly virtualized) used for processing, data storage, and similar purposes.	
System Software	Software that provides or contributes to an environment for storing, executing, and using software or data deployed within it.	
Equipment	A physical machine, tool, instrument, or livestock.	
Facility	A physical structure or environment.	
Communicatio n Network	A set of IT structures for transmission, routing, and reception of data.	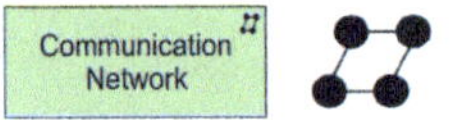
Distribution Network	A physical network used to transport materials or energy.	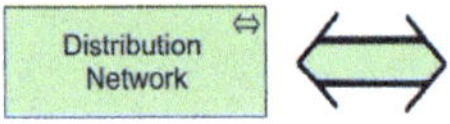

Element	Definition	Notation
Artifact	A piece of data that is used or produced in a software development process, or by deployment and operation of an IT system.	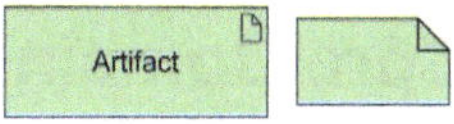
Material	Tangible physical matter or energy.	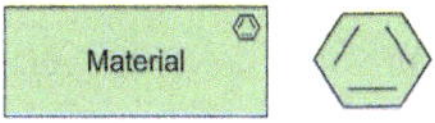

Chapter 10. Relationships Between Core Domains

This chapter describes the relationships that the ArchiMate language offers to model the link between business, applications, and technology.

Figure 10-1 shows the relationships between the Business, Application, and Technology Domain elements.

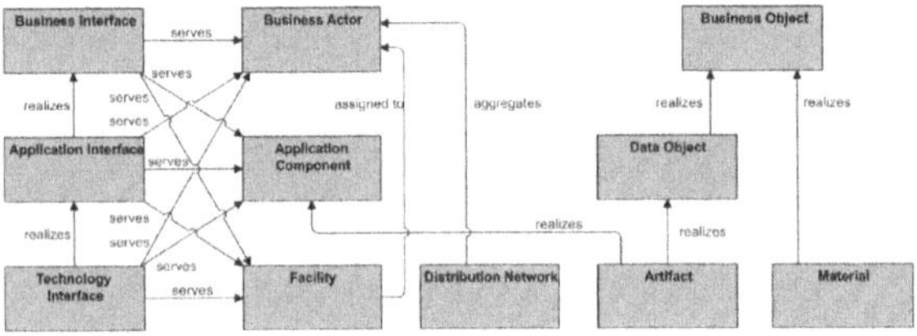

Figure 10-1: Relationships Between Business, Application, and Technology Domain Elements

There are three types of relationships between these domains; as specified here:

1. *Assignment*: From facility to business actor, typically used to indicate that people, teams, or other organization units work in a building
2. *Realization* relationships: For example, to indicate that a data object is a digital representation of the business object it realizes; that a business object is realized by material; that a data object is realized by a physical data file; or that a physical data file is an executable that realizes an application component
3. *Aggregation*: Business actors may be aggregated in distribution networks; for example, postal workers delivering mail as part of a mail distribution network

10.1. Example

Example 10-1 illustrates the insurance claims processing system at "ArchiSurance"; how customer claims, from initial registration through final payment, are handled.

The process begins when the "Customer", acting as an "Insurant", submits a claim through the "Claims Registration" system. This triggers a sequential workflow: "Register" → "Accept" → "Adjudicate" → "Pay". Three of these steps offer a corresponding service ("Claim Registration", "Claim Acceptance", and "Claim Payment") with which the "Insurant" interacts throughout the process.

The process is supported by two main applications: a "Financial Application" that handles "Payment Processing", and a "CRM System" for "Customer Data Management". These applications run on the "Blade System" hardware platform, which hosts "Application Server" and "Database Management System" system software.

The "Customer Information" flows through multiple layers — from "Customer Database Tables" through application-level "Customer Data" objects, to business-level "Customer Information" that the registration process can update. The "CRM System" has read-write access to "Customer Data", while the "Database Management" service maintains the underlying "Customer Database Tables".

Key technology artifacts include the "Database Access Java Archive" implementation for database access (supporting the "CRM System") and the "Financial Application" implementation, where the first is deployed on the "Database Management System" and the second on the "Application Server" infrastructure. The "Application Hosting" and "Database Management" services provide the foundational technology services that support the application components.

The entire system enables the "Insurer" role (fulfilled by ArchiSurance staff) to process a claim efficiently while maintaining proper data access controls and process flow from initial customer contact through final payment processing.

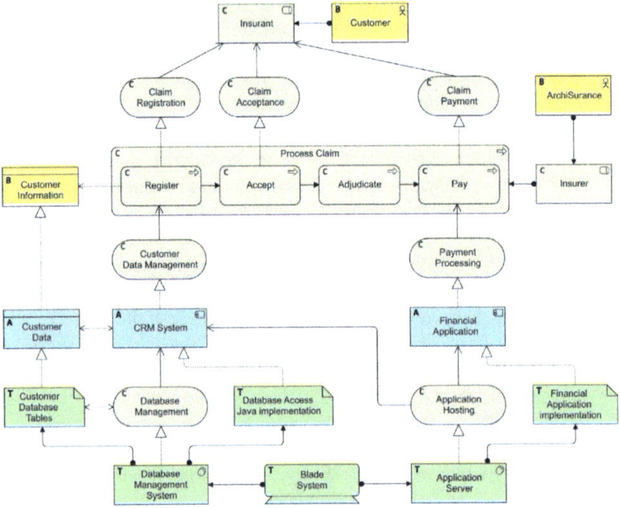

Example 10-1: Cross-Domain Relationships

Letters in the top-left corner of elements are used here to denote to which domain those elements belong, as described in Section 2.4.

Chapter 11. Implementation and Migration Domain

The implementation and migration elements support the implementation and migration of architectures.

11.1. Metamodel

The implementation and migration metamodel (see Figure 11-1) gives an overview of the implementation and migration elements and their relationships.

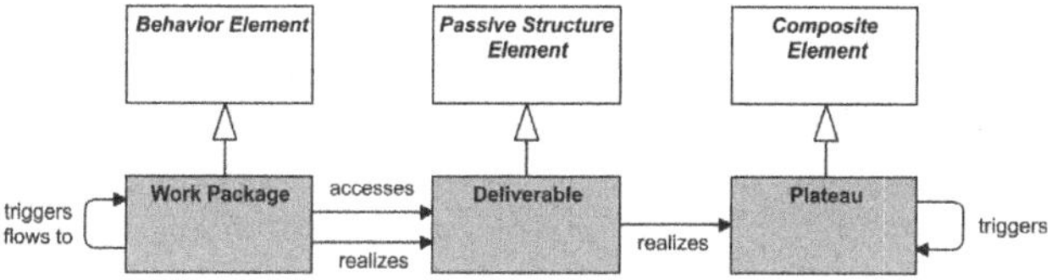

Figure 11-1: Implementation and Migration Metamodel

11.2. Elements

11.2.1. Work Package

> A work package represents a series of actions identified and designed to achieve specific results within specified time and resource constraints.

A work package is typically not a continuously ongoing activity, but has a start and an end. It produces a well-defined set of results, typically modeled as goals, outcomes, or deliverables. The work package element can be used to model sub-projects or tasks within a project, complete projects, programs, or project portfolios. In an Agile context, a work package can be used to model the work performed in an Agile iteration (e.g., sprint) or higher level increment.

Figure 11-2: Work Package Notation

11.2.2. Deliverable

A deliverable represents a result of a work package.

Work packages produce *deliverables*. These may be results of any kind; e.g., reports, papers, services, software, physical products, etc., or intangible results such as organizational change. A deliverable may also be the implementation of (a part of) an architecture. Often, deliverables are contractually specified and in turn formally reviewed, agreed, and signed off by the stakeholders as is; for example, prescribed by the TOGAF Standard [C220].

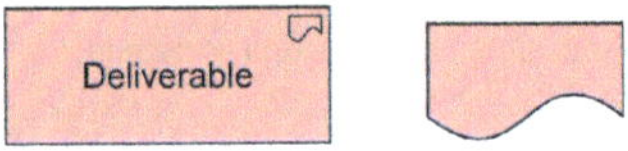

Figure 11-3: Deliverable Notation

11.2.3. Plateau

A plateau represents a relatively stable state of the architecture that exists during a limited period of time.

An important premise in the TOGAF framework is that the various architectures are described for different stages in time. In each of the Phases B, C, and D of the TOGAF Architecture Development Method (ADM), Baseline and Target Architecture Descriptions are created, describing the current situation and the desired future situation. In Phase E (Opportunities and Solutions), so-called Transition Architectures are defined, showing the enterprise at incremental states reflecting periods of transition between the Baseline and Target Architectures.

Transition Architectures are used to allow for individual work packages and projects to be grouped into managed portfolios and programs, illustrating the business value at each stage and expressing the step-by-step approach to migration.

In order to support this, the *plateau* element is defined.

Figure 11-4: Plateau Notation

11.2.4. Example

The "Next Generation Services Program" work package aggregates three other work packages. An event "Program Approved" triggers the first work package, "Architecture and Planning", which triggers the work package "Application Services Layer Development", which triggers the work package "Business Services Development", which in turn triggers the event "Program Completed". The "Program Approved" event also provides a deliverable "Program Brief", as input for the first work package. Work package "Architecture and Planning" realizes three deliverables: "Business Plan", "Architecture", and "Roadmap" (which is accessed by the "Application Services Layer Development" work package), which collectively realize the plateau "Strategic Plan Complete". This plateau follows the initial plateau "Baseline". Similarly, the other work packages realize other deliverables that realize the subsequent plateaus.

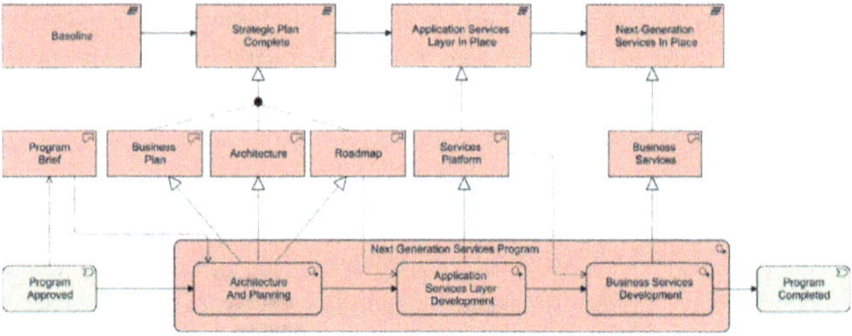

Example 11-1: Implementation and Migration Elements

11.3. Summary

Table 11-1 provides a summary of the implementation and migration elements, with their definitions.

Table 11-1: Implementation and Migration Elements

Element	Definition	Notation
Work Package	A series of actions identified and designed to achieve specific results within specified time and resource constraints.	
Deliverable	A result of a work package.	
Plateau	A relatively stable state of the architecture that exists during a limited period of time.	

Chapter 12. Architecture Views and Viewpoints

12.1. Introduction

The ArchiMate language provides a flexible approach in which architects and other stakeholders can use their own views on the Enterprise Architecture. In this approach, architecture views are specified by architecture viewpoints. Architecture viewpoints define abstractions on the set of models representing the Enterprise Architecture, each aimed at a particular type of stakeholder and addressing a particular set of concerns. Viewpoints can be used to view certain aspects in isolation, and also to relate two or more aspects.

12.2. Architecture Views and Viewpoints

Architecture views are an ideal mechanism to purposefully convey information about architecture areas. In general, a view is defined as a part of an Architecture Description that addresses a set of related concerns and is tailored for specific stakeholders. A view is specified by means of an architecture viewpoint, which prescribes the concepts, models, analysis techniques, and visualizations that are provided by the view. Simply put, a view is what you see, and a viewpoint is where you are looking from.

An Architecture Description includes one or more architecture views. An architecture view (or simply "view") addresses one or more of the concerns held by a stakeholder of the system.

An architecture view expresses the architecture of the system of interest in accordance with an architecture viewpoint (or simply "viewpoint"). There are two aspects to a viewpoint: the concerns it frames for the stakeholders and the conventions it establishes on views.

An architecture viewpoint frames one or more concerns. A concern can be framed by more than one viewpoint.

A view is governed by its viewpoint: the viewpoint establishes the conventions for constructing, interpreting, and analyzing the view to address concerns framed by that viewpoint. Viewpoint conventions can include languages, notations, model kinds, design rules and/or modeling methods, analysis techniques, and other operations on views.

Architecture viewpoints are a means to focus on particular aspects and domains of the architecture. These aspects and domains are determined by the concerns of a stakeholder with whom communication takes place. What should and should not be visible from a specific viewpoint is therefore entirely dependent on the argumentation with respect to a stakeholder's concerns.

Viewpoints are designed for the purpose of communicating certain aspects and domains of an architecture. The communication enabled by a viewpoint can be strictly informative, but in general is bi-directional. The architect informs stakeholders, and stakeholders give their feedback (critique or consent) on the presented aspects and domains. What is and what is not shown in an architecture view depends on the scope of the viewpoint and on what is relevant to the concerns of the stakeholder. Ideally, these are the same; i.e., the viewpoint is designed with specific concerns of a stakeholder in mind. Relevance to a stakeholder's concern, therefore, is the selection criterion that is used to determine which elements and relationships are to appear in a view.

12.3. Viewpoint Mechanism

An architect is confronted with many different types of stakeholders and concerns. To help in selecting the right viewpoints for the task at hand, the specification includes a framework for the definition and classification of viewpoints: the *viewpoint mechanism*. The framework is based on two dimensions: purpose and content. Figure 12-1 shows how the viewpoint mechanism is used to create views addressing stakeholder concerns.

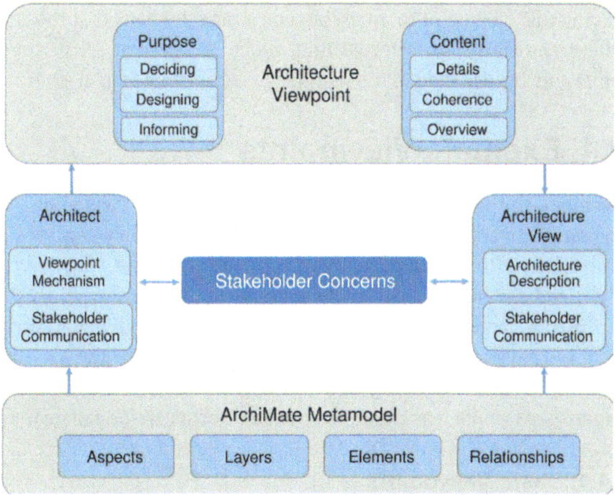

Figure 12-1: Framing Stakeholder Concerns using the Viewpoint Mechanism

The architect communicates with the stakeholder to understand and document their concerns. The viewpoint mechanism is used to identify purpose and content and to help define and classify the viewpoint. The viewpoint governs the construction and design of the view. The view is a description of the architecture addressing stakeholder concerns and is governed by the viewpoint.

Creating an ArchiMate viewpoint consists of two steps:

1. Selecting a subset of relevant concepts (elements and relationships) from the ArchiMate metamodel, based on the information that is needed to address the stakeholder's concerns

2. Defining a representation to depict these concepts in a way that is understood by the stakeholders

   This can be a diagram that uses standard or customized ArchiMate notation, a catalog of elements, a matrix showing the relationships between two groups of elements, or an entirely different visualization.

Applying this viewpoint to an architecture model means that those parts of the architecture are selected that match the chosen set of concepts (Step 1) and are depicted in the manner prescribed by Step 2.

12.4. Example Viewpoints

Appendix C of the standard provides a set of example viewpoints. These viewpoints are starting points for modeling efforts. They can accelerate architectural efforts, support organizational standards, facilitate peer review, and aid new modelers. However, these basic viewpoints should not constrain modeling activities. Organizations and individual modelers should address stakeholder concerns by selecting from the viewpoints, modifying them, or defining new ones. The viewpoints defined in the standard are intended as examples, not as a normative or exhaustive list.

12.4.1. Basic Viewpoints

Based on common architectural practice and on experiences with the use of ArchiMate models in practical cases, useful combinations in the form of a set of basic viewpoints are defined in the standard. These are listed in Table 12-1. The table also shows the perspective for the viewpoint. Some viewpoints have a scope that is limited to a single domain or aspect, when others link multiple domains and/or aspects. The different viewpoints are grouped into categories that indicate which direction and which elements the viewpoint is looking at:

1. *Composition*: Viewpoints that define the internal structure of elements
2. *Support*: Viewpoints where you are looking at elements that are supported by other elements
3. *Cooperation*: Toward peer elements that cooperate with each other, typically across aspects
4. *Realization*: Viewpoints where you are looking at elements that realize other elements

Table 12-1: Basic Viewpoints

Category: Composition		
Name	**Perspective**	**Scope**
Organization	Structure of the enterprise in terms of roles, departments, etc.	Single domain, single aspect
Application Structure	Shows the structure of a typical application in terms of its constituents	Single domain, multiple aspects
Information Structure	Shows the structure of the information used in the enterprise	Multiple domains, single aspects
Technology	Infrastructure and platforms underlying the enterprise's information systems in terms of networks, devices, and system software	Single domain, multiple aspects
Layered	Provides overview of architecture(s)	Multiple domains, multiple aspects
Physical	Physical environment and how this relates to IT infrastructure	Multiple domains, multiple aspects
Category: Support		
Name	**Perspective**	**Scope**
Product	Shows the contents of products	Multiple domains, multiple aspects
Application Usage	Relates applications to their use in, for example, processes	Multiple domains, multiple aspects
Technology Usage	Shows how technology is used by applications	Multiple domains, multiple aspects
Category: Cooperation		
Name	**Perspective**	**Scope**
Process Cooperation	Shows the relationships between various processes	Multiple domains, multiple aspects
Application Cooperation	Shows application components and their mutual relationships	Application Domain, multiple aspects

Category: Realization		
Name	**Perspective**	**Scope**
Service Realization	Shows how services are realized by the requisite behavior	Multiple domains, multiple aspects
Implementation and Deployment	Shows how applications are mapped onto the underlying technology	Multiple domains, multiple aspects

12.4.2. Motivation Viewpoints

The following viewpoints to support modeling motivational aspects of the enterprise are defined in the standard:

- The *stakeholder viewpoint* focuses on modeling the stakeholders, drivers, the assessments of these drivers, and the initial goals to address these drivers and assessments
- The *goal realization viewpoint* focuses on refining the initial, high-level goals into more concrete (sub-)goals using the aggregation relationship, and finally into requirements using the realization relationship
- The *goal contribution viewpoint* focuses on modeling and analyzing the influence relationships between goals (and requirements)
- The *principles viewpoint* focuses on modeling the relevant principles and the goals that motivate these principles
- The *requirements realization viewpoint* focuses on modeling the realization of requirements by means of core elements, such as actors, services, processes, application components, etc.
- The *motivation viewpoint* covers the entire motivational aspect and allows use of all motivational elements

12.4.3. Strategy Viewpoints

The following viewpoints for modeling strategic aspects of the enterprise are defined in the standard:

- The *strategy viewpoint* provides a high-level strategic overview of the strategies of the enterprise, its capabilities, value streams, and resources, and the envisaged outcomes
- The *capability map viewpoint* provides an overview of the capabilities of the enterprise
- The *value stream viewpoint* shows an overview of value-creating steps in the enterprise and the capabilities that support these
- The *outcome realization viewpoint* describes how high-level, business-oriented results are produced by the capabilities and resources of the enterprise
- The *resource map viewpoint* provides a structured overview of the resources of the enterprise

12.4.4. Implementation and Migration Viewpoints

The following viewpoints for modeling implementation and migration aspects are defined in the standard:

- The *project viewpoint* is primarily used to model the management of architecture change
- The *migration viewpoint* is used to model the transition from an existing architecture to a Target Architecture
- The *implementation and migration viewpoint* is used to model the relationships between the programs and projects and the parts of the architecture that they implement

Appendix A: Language Notation Summary

This appendix describes the default iconography of the ArchiMate language.

Core Elements

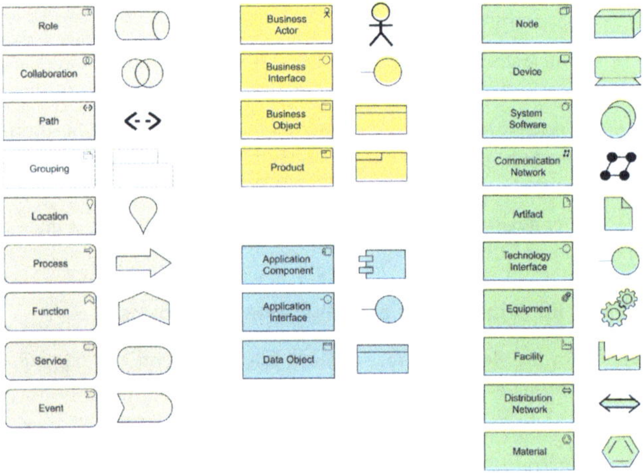

Motivation, Strategy, Implementation and Migration Elements

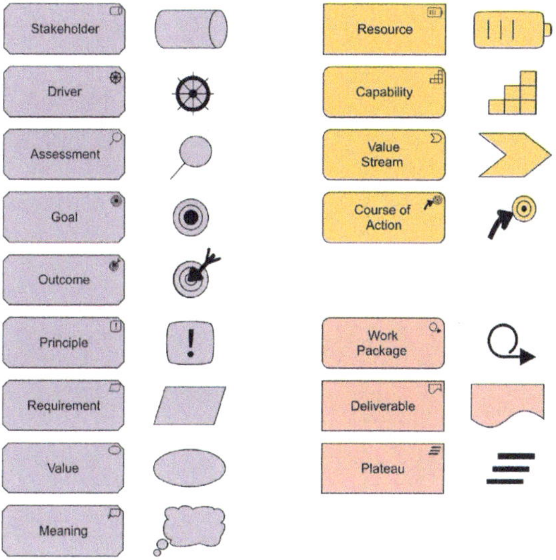

Relationships and Junctions

Appendix B: Referenced Documents

The following documents are referenced in this document. These references are informative.

(Please note that the links below are good at the time of writing but cannot be guaranteed for the future.)

[C220] TOGAF® Standard, 10th Edition, a standard of The Open Group (C220), published by The Open Group, April 2022 and updated May 2025 to include Technical Corrigendum 1; refer to: www.opengroup.org/library/c220

[C260] ArchiMate® 4 Specification, a standard of The Open Group (C260), published by The Open Group, April 2026; refer to: www.opengroup.org/library/c260

[G21E] How to Use the ArchiMate® Modeling Language to Support the TOGAF® Standard, The Open Group Guide (G21E), published by The Open Group, April 2022; refer to: www.opengroup.org/library/g21e

Appendix C: Glossary

ArchiMate Core Language

The central part of the ArchiMate language that defines the core elements to model Enterprise Architectures. It includes elements from four domains: Common, Business, Application, and Technology.

ArchiMate Full Language

The full content of the ArchiMate language that defines all elements that can be used to model Enterprise Architectures. It includes elements from the following domains: Motivation, Strategy, Common, Business, Application, Technology, and Implementation and Migration.

Architecture Domain

A grouping construct used to structure architectural descriptions into broad areas such as Business, Application, Technology, Motivation, Strategy, and Implementation & Migration.

Architecture View

A representation of a system from the perspective of a related set of concerns.

Architecture Viewpoint

A specification of the conventions for a particular kind of architecture view.

Aspect

Classification of elements based on domain-independent characteristics related to the concerns of different stakeholders. Used for positioning elements in the ArchiMate metamodel.

Attribute

A property associated with an ArchiMate language concept.

Composite Element

Unlike elements from the active structure, behavior, and passive structure aspects, composite elements are collections of concepts that can be from multiple aspects of the language.

Concept

Either an element, a relationship, or a junction.

Core Element

An element in one of the core domains (Common Domain, Business Domain, Application Domain, or Technology Domain) of the ArchiMate language.

Domain

A subset of the ArchiMate language for modeling specific characteristics of an enterprise and its architecture.

Element

Basic unit in the ArchiMate metamodel. Used to define and describe the constituent parts of Enterprise Architectures and their unique set of characteristics.

Model

A collection of concepts in the context of the ArchiMate language structure.

Relationship

A connection between a source and target concept. Classified as structural, dependency, dynamic, or other.

Index

Made in the USA
Coppell, TX
04 November 2026

11269351R00075